POETRY REVIEW

WINTER 2000/2001 VOLUME 90 NUMBER 4

EDITOR PETER FORBES
PRODUCTION JANET PHILLIPS
ADVERTISING LISA ROBERTS

CONTENTS

Illustrations by Gerald Mangan

Stand

BRITAIN'S FOREMOST LITERARY QUARTERLY

EDITORS
Michael Hulse
John Kinsella

EDITORIAL OFFICE
School of English
University of Leeds
Leeds LS2 9JT
PH: +44 (0) 113 233 4794
FAX: +44 (0) 113 233 4791
EMAIL: stand@english.novell.
leeds.ac.uk
WEBSITE: http://saturn.vcu.
edu/-dlatane/stand.html

SUBSCRIPTIONS
WorldWide Subscriptions
Unit 4, Gibbs Reed Farm,
Ticehurst, E. Sussex,
TN5 7HE
ph:+44 (0)1580 200 657
fax:+44 (0)1580 200 616

SUBSCRIPTION RATES
One Year: £25.00 (UK)
Student/Unwaged: £18.00
Single copy (by mail): £7.00

IN SEPTEMBER 2000

New work from New Zealand writers including Barbara Anderson, Lauris Edmond, Charlotte Grimshaw, Vincent O'Sullivan and Elizabeth Smither. Plus poetry by Charles Boyle and Sheenagh Pugh, fiction by Brian Howell, and Glyn Maxwell's *ars poetica*.

IN MARCH 2001,

NOBEL PRIZE ISSUE

In partnership with *The Kenyon Review*, a major issue celebrating the first century of the Nobel Prize, to mark and accompany the Nobel Museum's exhibition as it begins four years travelling the world.

"IF YOU WANT THE EXCITEMENT OF ORIGINAL LITERARY ACHIEVEMENT, OF A PASSION FOR IT, I RECOMMEND *STAND*." RICHARD HOLMES

POETRY REVIEW SUBSCRIPTIONS
Four issues including postage:

UK individuals £27
Overseas individuals £35
(all overseas delivery is by airmail)
USA individuals $56

Libraries, schools and institutions:
UK £35
Overseas £42
USA $66

Single issue £6.95 + 50p p&p (UK)

Sterling and US dollar payments only.
Eurocheques, Visa and Mastercard payments are acceptable.

Bookshop distribution:
Signature
Telephone 0161 834 8767

Design by Philip Lewis
Cover by Janet Phillips
Cover image © PhotoDisc, Inc

Typeset by Poetry Review.

Printed by Newnorth Print Ltd at Newnorth House, College Street Kempston, Bedford MK42 8NA
Telephone: 01234 341111

POETRY REVIEW is the magazine of the Poetry Society. It is published quarterly and issued free to members of the Poetry Society. Poetry Review considers submissions from non-members and members alike. To ensure reply submissions must be accompanied by an SAE or adequate International Reply coupons: Poetry Review accepts no responsibility for contributions that are not reply paid.

Founded 24 February 1909
Charity Commissioners No: 303334
© 2001

EDITORIAL AND BUSINESS ADDRESS:
22 BETTERTON STREET, LONDON WC2H 9BX

telephone   **020 7420 9880**   fax **020 7240 4818**
email   **poetryreview@poetrysoc.com**   ISBN **1 900771 23 3**
website   **http://www.poetrysoc.com**   ISSN **0032 2156**

The Poetry Society
is supported by
BT

Changing Places

ALASTAIR NIVEN ON RECENT SOUTH ASIAN POETRY

ARVIND KRISHNA MEHROTRA

The Transfiguring Places

Sangam Books, £6.95
ISBN 81 7530 019 1

ALAMGIR HASHMI

A Choice of Hashmi's Verse

OUP Pakistan, £9.95
ISBN 0 19 577813 8

M.ATHAR TAHIR

A Certain Season

OUP Pakistan, £10
ISBN 0 19 579189 4

KETAKI KUSHARI DYSON

Memories of Argentina and other poems

Virgilio Libris, 62 Banbury Road, Oxford OX5 1AH
£7.95 plus £1 p&p
ISBN 0 95370520 X

AGHA SHAHID ALI

The Country Without a Post Office

Norton, £8.50
ISBN 0 393 31761 7

BIBHU PADHI

Burning the House

Sangam, £3.95
ISBN 0 86311796 1

VIJAY SESHADRI

Wild Kingdom

Graywolf Press, £10.99
ISBN 1 55597 236 5

Nine Indian Women Poets

Edited by Eunice de Souza

OUP India, £15
ISBN 0 19 564077 2

The Redbeck Anthology of British South Asian Poetry

Edited by Debjani Chatterjee

Redbeck, £9.95
ISBN 0 946980 76 4

WHEN TEN BOOKS of poetry from the Indian sub-continent land on one's desk there seems to be evidence bearing out William Walsh's much quoted remark of twenty or more years ago, that though the present strength of Indian literature in English might lie with its fiction its future would be with its poetry. Walsh was appointed the first Professor of Commonwealth Literature in Britain (or Post-colonial Literature, as such posts are now styled, if not New Literatures in English, or International Literature, or Anglophone Writing, or the Uncle Tom Cobbley Chair of Total Inclusiveness). India was his special area, so his prophecy is worth taking seriously. It seemed in the decade or so after he wrote this, that he was right. Arun Kolatkar, Arun Joshi, Gieve Patel, Jayanta Mahapatra, Meena Alexander, Eunice de Souza, and many others emerged, winning some awards and suggesting that a vibrant poetic voice was escaping from the apparent stranglehold of the indigenous mother tongues.

Now, however, the picture looks rather different. There is growing awareness of the quality of Indian poetry in many of the country's seventeen official languages. Far too little of this has yet been translated, but poets are beginning to be known outside their immediate language group. Although the occasional Vikram Seth has broken through to wider recognition, almost no new poet has won the laurels of Kolatkar and his peers either in the sub-continent itself or elsewhere. This crop of books, therefore, is a bit of a test to discover if the talent is there, merely awaiting the attention of *Poetry Review* before it leaps to celebrity.

Much the best-known of the writers here is Arvind Krishna Mehrotra. *The Transfiguring Places* is his fourth collection, though he is also the author of a collection of translations, *The Absent Traveller*, and the influential editor of *The Oxford India Anthology of Twelve Modern Indian Poets*, Mehrotra's technical skills are here displayed with great versatility. He seldom repeats the same arrangement of verses or metrical formation, though everything is always highly ordered. In a six-stanza poem composed of five tetraines and a quatraine, apparently describing a street killing, he repeats two lines, "I cannot live here all my life" and "A quiet man pulls out a knife", so that they acquire the insistence of a mantra. This yoking together of casual violence in a social setting with great formality of technique may be at times austere, but it is poetically very rewarding. On every page one knows one is encountering a real talent.

Mehrotra's is a bleak and often sardonic view of the world:

Sometimes,
In unwiped bathroom mirrors,
He sees all three faces
Looking at him:

His own,
The grey-haired man's
Whose life policy has matured,
And the mocking youth's
Who paid the first premium.

('Approaching Fifty')

This self-detachment runs through the work. In many poems Mehrotra casts himself as an almost Jamesian observer, watching the small niceties of other people's bleak ephemeral existences. We have a record here more of the poet's seeing eye than his feeling heart, so that the combination of formal craft and quiet witnessing can create an almost frosty effect. In poem after poem phrases underscore the watching brief that the poet seems to set himself: "View the passing show with an inward eye", "the sight / Of common birds in exuberant flight", "I look at your hiding places again", "I saw him last / Who passes before me / In the cheval-glass", "Watching postmen go past the front gate / With nothing for me", "Unaware of the wide-eyed passers-by", "Unable to see you in the failing light".

In 'Nautical, 1' Mehrotra catches the fleeting contact of our daily brushes with the world of strangers in which we all live.

Those jetty lights are wax candles
Flickering over bald cabbages.
At makeshift stalls behind
The Accountant General's Office,

Gray-stubbled, fecund, homebound clerks –
Their lastborn the same age
As their first grandchild –
Haggle for perishables.

Harsh but ephemeral struggles for survival, moments of tenderness in an unforgiving life, these characterise Mehrotra's outlook. 'Nautical, 1' continues:

Their frenzied voices roll and heave
As she comes into view, vanishes,
Reappears, weighed down by stout canvas
Shopping bags, and squeezing
The car keys in her hand.
She comes alongside,
And for what seems a long time,
Out of the corner of her eye
Watches me watching her buy
Cucumbers and spring onions.

Mehrotra is a writer in full flood, drawing every now and then on a classical source in Indian or European literature (I suspect that Catullus, whom he names in one poem, is a big influence). There is not a weak poem in the book. Yet I doubt if there is a great one either. This is a poet of consummate craft and with a vision apt for these times, but in the end his work avoids major challenges. Its precision of language is a joy and poets in particular will relish the handful of poems here which specifically address the craft of writing:

Last night a line appeared,
Unbidden, unsigned;
It had eight memorable
Syllables. I'll keep you,

I said, falling asleep.
It's gone now,
And I write this to requite it,
And to mark its passage.

('Inscription')

Sadly, there is no other collection here in the same class. Alamgir Hashmi is the longest established poet among the single author volumes, but the slightly fey title, *A Choice of Hashmi's Verse*, hints at some soft-centred writing:

It proposes itself

in so many ways
to the soul riveted
to autumn's fading bough:
love is what you can't
live with,
and keep trying
to get back to;
green changing back
to green in the tint
of intervals.'

('How to Say Goodbye')

Hashmi has given good service to poetry of the sub-continent over thirty-five years; indeed, he was for a long time the only Pakistani poet writing in English with any sort of international reputation. He can produce the witty unexpected phrase ("Tibet reads in Urdu / like tit") or the plangent moment ("Our looks fill in / the vacancy of eyes, / and night waits / on the stars falling in your hair"), but there is too much etiolated versifying here, as though freshness of perception was being stood up by literary duty.

M.Athar Tahir is also Pakistani. *A Certain Season* takes us through many landscapes, often with energy and a real concern for form. Though Auden, Blake and Kipling are invoked, much of the collection is rooted in Iqbal and earlier indigenous traditions. This is a fine collection, but Tahir still seems to be experimenting with voices rather sounding one of his own.

This is the problem with the remaining poets here. Each is capable of great beauty, but too often monotony sets in because self-discipline is sacrificed to a desire to express everything all in one go. Ketaki Kushari Dyson is learned, wide-ranging and often lyrical, with a vigorous dramatic quality (her latest work is a stage play). Too often, though, she over-writes and the reader drifts away. The same is true of Agha Shahid Ali, who mixes prose poems with long disquisitions on fate and time. *The Country Without a Post Office* provides, however, the closest poetic view we have recently had of Kashmir and its continuing political ordeal. Tabish Khair is a very physical writer, his poems full of action and description, like small stories. Though sometimes clumsy, Khair is fully engaged with experience. There is nothing rarified about him and the poems amply re-pay a second visit.

Bibhu Padhi's poetry is infused with a sense of loss. Awareness of transience, perhaps especially of

art and talent, seeps into several poems here:

'Today we shall talk of the small things.
Of your steadily failing hold
on the modest words on your hands,
in your small hands.
Of how, yesterday, the hand failed to write.'

('The Captive Hand')

There is very little local detail here. Padhi writes of ancient themes, grief, longing, belief, mortality, but in the end his poems have a slightly sweet, even cloying, effect, like the smell of death.

I prefer the pacey in-your-face realism of Vijay Seshadri. *Wild Kingdom* is not an especially original book, but it is populated with real people. In the main these are American urban poems ("I heard two shots as I slipped out across / 138th Street…"), with a strong narrative drive. Seshadri is the least "sub-continental" poet among these collections, to such an extent that it would probably not occur to a reader who did not recognise the derivation of his name that the author was born in India. He is, however, a writer to watch, vigorously linking a contemplative mind with inner-city realities.

Eunice de Souza includes herself in her anthology *Nine Indian Women Poets*, which is just as well because she is one of the most fastidious and yet wickedly sharp poets I know. There is not space to do justice to this collection, which is already being used widely in Indian colleges. It contains the big feminine voices of modern India, including Kamala Das, Imtiaz Dharker and Sujata Bhatt, as well as less familiar names. It deserves a full review to itself.

So does *The Redbeck Anthology of British South Asian Poetry*. Perhaps this is the most variable collection of the ten I bring together here, but that is because it is a pioneering work and seeks to record a seismic cultural shift in British poetry. There have been other anthologies of black and Asian writing in Britain, but none as targeted as this. Here in one collection are not only many names likely to be familiar with readers of *Poetry Review* (for example, Romesh Gunesekera, Moniza Alvi and Suniti Namjoshi) but fifty or so with whom most of us are not familiar. Definitions are arbitrary, which allows the Guyanese David Dabydeen to be included, but this is a book bursting with vitality. Debjani Chatterjee has edited a collection of some historic import, the only one reviewed here which represents a true break-through.

The Leafing Lotus Bed

by Smita Agarwal

THE EROTIC IS an energetic and enjoyable presence in Indian art and literature. If there isn't much by way of the erotic in contemporary Indian verse in English is this because poetry in English in India is a relatively new tradition less than 200 years old? Why have Indian poets writing in English shied away from exploring and exploiting the erotic? Is the historical accident of colonial conquest a reason for the poets being hampered by an Old Testament morality?

The erotic is a problematic zone. Usually, an erotic poem is personal, meant for one, and mostly embarrassing reading for others. It's difficult to write, as Eros tends to duck beneath thick symbolic armour – using conscious or unconscious shields to come between desire and its representation.

A good erotic poem will express desire; incite desire. The successful erotic poem will lead on to that moment when passion in extremis transforms...

Nissim Ezekiel's audacious 'Nudes 1978' in free verse talks candidly of lust. The poet's sense of the comic enables the reader to denude and demythologize the romantic padding around an act of desire:

> "Is this a part of you?" she asks,
> as she holds it, stares at it.
> Then she laughs. "Put your finger
> there", she pleads, as if
> I need instructions...

So it works, but only just. Ezekiel is as usual wordy and abstruse. He can't resist the tendency to philosophise:

> ...The verbal
> and the visual join in her.

> Long before Arundhati Roy in prose, Kamala Das wrote of desire in poetry with candour, vigour, self-assurance and grace, much to the discomfiture of queasy, mostly male, academic critics in India

Ezekiel's earlier show of skill 'Poet, Lover, Birdwatcher' stokes desire via indirection and suggestion. It's a layered poem where the pun on birdwatching twines around poet and lover. After patient watching and waiting there's a barely perceptible, discreet chase which leads to surrender and to that moment when "the deaf can hear, the blind recover sight".

In the sixteenth century, the Hindi poet Surdas, writing in a religious mode, spoke of similar miracles made possible by God's grace when

> ...the mute may speak
> the lame leap over mountains...

Although high-sounding notes like –

> In this the poet finds his moral proved,
> Who never spoke before his spirit moved.

– disturb my sense of contemporary idiom, and abstract descriptions like –

> Not only flesh and bone but myths of light
> With darkness at the core...

– make me impatient, nevertheless, I can't help feel that in 'Poet, Lover, Birdwatcher' Ezekiel has come close to using the symbols of sex to give voice to something else: some sort of an ultimate Eros that is fundamental, mythical and unattainable. A.K. Ramanujan's 'Love 5' (8-22 February 1993) is a sonnet: an erotic poem with the human touch. It races on in bed – flashing lightning, stripping stark naked, not waiting for the half-dark, rising and falling, saying "unspeakable things to her back and front", tasting "her juices at their sources", stoking "the smithy all hours to hammer rings" etc. – to that stunning moment of daylight when the night-stud metamorphoses into an embarrassed adolescent, stammering and shy.

Long before Arundhati Roy in prose, Kamala Das wrote of desire in poetry with candour, vigour, self-assurance and grace, much to the discomfiture of queasy, mostly male, academic critics in India. Her middle-class, middle-aged persona could express bewilderment at the efforts of a boorish husband and choose to drive her "blue battered car" "…to knock at another's door" and repeat rhetorically:

> …ask me why he is called a lion,
> …ask me the flavour of his
> Mouth, ask me why his hand sways like a hooded
> > snake
>
> Before it clasps my pubis…
> …. ask me what is bliss…

Years later, a younger Sujata Bhatt writing from the outside finishes with *élan* what Das may have started. Eunice de Souza in *Nine Indian Women Poets* calls Bhatt's poem "the only successful erotic poem in Indian writing in English".

In Bhatt's 'White Asparagus', a pregnant woman in her fourth month is caught off-guard by desire. She wants him to

> ….come like a horse,
> move like a dog, a wolf,
> become a suckling lion-cub –
>
> Come here, and here, and here –
> but swim fast and don't stop.

The poem pulls in the reader as "even the smell pulls her in". 'White Asparagus' succeeds because Bhatt is able to find the exact metaphor for heterosexual-female sexual hunger – "sun-deprived white and purple-shadow veined" asparagus, "some so jauntily capped".

'The Round of the Seasons (In the footsteps of Abhinanda and Yogeswara)' by Keki N. Daruwalla connects with an older tradition, an older canon. Daruwalla's translations of Sanskrit poets has helped him get this poem. It's a long one in six sections, each section representing a season. Whereas in the Ezekiel and Ramanujan poems the setting is urban, the tone urbane, in this one the landscape is rural, the tone rustic. Yogeswara was a Sanskrit poet active in the court of the Pala dynasty in Eastern India. He lived no later than the ninth

century, and is best known for his realistic depictions of nature and peasant life. Abhinanda too was an easterner writing at the time of the Pala dynasty. Culled from the *Natyashastra* and the Sanskrit poetic tradition, Daruwalla's poem brings into play in English, *nayika bhed* (female personality types) and *dhvani* (suggestion). Both these devices are not unknown in other languages but, Sanskrit poets use *dhvani* with brilliance to convey excitement.

> It is the season for illusions.
> …
> A bird alights on the leafing lotus bed
> thinking it is an island.
> Bathing on the ghats,
> shawled in mist, she finds
> bees moving towards her breast-tips.

Daruwalla's poem lets us see how, if well done, modern English, a lean language with an ironic underpinning, may be made more voluptuous without losing sight of its grammatical bone and sinew.

Leaving behind Daruwalla's Indian landscape, the erotic imagination of the Indian poet writing in English shifts location and swoops down to prey on the geography and culture of Mexico.

Dom Moraes' 'Mexico Perhaps' is a 58 year-old man's poem – staccato sentences and moving images:

> Morning opens its mouth.
> …
> Thorns clatter as the rattlesnake dies
> …
> Light falls level on empty altars.
> …
> The extinct volcano, maned with snow,
> rears over you, but will roar no more.

An autumnal desert landscape, silence, sluggishness, snow, death, whiteness are imagistically juxtaposed with lusciousness, wetness:

> Darknippled, heavy, your breasts
> taste of lost orchards.

More a poem of intense longing and loss, than of lust and conquest, 'Mexico Perhaps' revolves around the inability to translate desire into action. Its dreamlike quality makes it a fine example of the correlation between the imagination and the erotic. To what extent is the erotic moment an imagined moment? Do erotic sentiments, if they exist at all, live and die in the mind?

Part Three of Eunice de Souza's 'Outside Jaisalmer' has recourse to the tradition of Rajasthani miniature painting: "The life of the hero on the scabbard of a sword". De Souza uses a language of utmost clarity for description.

Faces in profile, erect penis in profile
the colours raw, the rug in detail:

At the moment of greatest tension:

He looks into her eyes
she looks into his.

De Souza veers off to describe the waiting women behind the lattice work, almost as if the end result could never be anything but inexpressible. Skillfully, in a short lyric of just nine lines de Souza succeeds in conveying and inciting erotic excitement:

He looks into her eyes
she looks into his.
Behind the lattice work the
waiting women
cry oh and stroke their
breasts.

Arvind Krishna Mehrotra's 'Nautical, 1' describes a scene: a busy marketplace, a person. Realistic documentation is a tool the poet uses to undercut emotional involvement. Within the drama of the poem the reader is unsure whether the poem is about passion at all – so cleverly is desire controlled. But the suggestive power of language wins as when, for the speaking voice looking on at

Gray-stubbled, fecund, home-bound clerks –
Their lastborn the same age
As their first grandchild –

cucumbers and spring onions emerge as Eliot-like erotic symbols of painful rejuvenation.

Nissim Ezekiel and A.K. Ramanujan at one end of the erotic spectrum, Jeet Thayil and Makarand Paranjape, post independence younger poets at the other, reveal how the language of sex and the function of the sign of sex has changed over the years. While the older poets assign positive values to the erotic encounter, the younger poets assign lower values of revulsion, grotesqueness, caricature and anticlimax.

Thayil's 'Working Girl' and Paranjape's 'Miss Gobble' are set in big cities with their potential for desexualization. The 'Working Girl' is a grotesque creature:

...Sumo woman
Sex wrestler, vast expanse of flesh agog,
Squatting on the raised platform of her bed,
Splayed on the raised platform of her sex;
She is completely certain of victory.

And, Miss Gobble, purveyor of pleasure, with whom the protagonist of the poem manages "To get so much done" bothers him with her "not too pleasant odour" which adds "to the squalor / Of your already sullied vocation..." Yet it is to Miss Gobble the protagonist goes, "carrying" his "awkward burden":

Of necessity
In you I seek relief ...

A poem that tackles both masturbation and fellatio and wherein the speaking voice confesses "heedless of repercussions, / I release myself to my utmost satisfaction" ends on a note of anticlimax:

Walking off, I leave you on the bench tidying-up.
Incidentally, your next client happens to be someone
I know, his room is opposite mine on the same floor.
Perhaps he'll drop in afterwards to compare notes.

Like any erotic poem, 'Miss Gobble' talks of desire, incites desire and leads up that alley where the ferocity of passion makes the poetic imagination transmogrify.

> The language of sex and the function of the sign of sex has changed over the years. While the older poets assign positive values to the erotic encounter, the younger poets assign lower values of revulsion, grotesqueness, caricature and anticlimax.

SMITA AGARWAL
PARROTS

What do you know
Of the fragrant oils
That seep out of her cells
At the sight of a pair
Of parrots in flight.

Jets of green, they arc,
Swerve, rise up and dive,
Dip and rise, alight
On a mango branch,
Sit side by side, and,
Thus arranged, proceed to
Peck at each others' necks –
Using their beaks like the
Teeth of a blood-red comb,
Groom each other, head to toe...

There... he's licking her throat,
Burying his head between her breasts,
He's suckling them like
Sucking on ripe mangoes...
Here, he's at her navel...
He's sloshing his tongue around...
He's turned her over...
Nips at the back of her shoulders,
Bites all down her spine,
Now, he's using his hands to knead her...

The parrots are beak to beak.
Her fragrant oils alight, she seeks
The metallic aroma of blue-black ink
Streaming on paper...
Her saliva has a sour, astringent taste...

TWO POEMS BY BUDDHADEVA BOSE (1908-74)
TO MEMORY: 1

It's you I accept as Goddess. There's nothing that's not yours.
What I call the well-spring, the root cause, is really your sleep:
intact even on the horizon, stealthily it creeps,
but if, half glancing, you turn in bed, a lush wonder flowers

and glossy grapes kiss the earth, turning it to wine.
So the canvas lies blank, stone's inert, the vina just a jarring whine
till you teach us how to cross the surf, navigate the main,
till you lead us beyond the track, the rugged terrain

of warring night and day, to eternity's peaceful plain,
from far to farther, to another birth, the prehistoric cerulean
where, in a matrix, like a cluster of stars, burn

man's destiny and your unending treasures.
Darkness is what you own, but greater than light is that dark,
and utterly valueless is what you idly discard.

(6-7 May 1955)

TO MEMORY: 2

"Tree", "flower", "pond", "cloudy day": are dry mathematical symbols,
merely abstract, till you raise the curtain and show that my eyes too are
yours.
The vine trails over my body, a field bursts into sudden yellow flowers,
dyeing the sky-line. And thus I come to claim the earth, stars, and all else.

War flares; the citizen runs abroad, roaming from shore to shore,
losing in an instant letters, pictures, manuscripts, all that cold store;
but still he won't lose you, for the pole star is your sign,
which never sets elsewhere and is of all hoards the inner gold mine.

On a straight road we walk. Ants in procession, along the diligent miles,
carry the corpse of a huge insect through childhood, the youthful years,
even dragging from age to age documents, signatures, files –

till gradually men's countless children grow old and disappear.

But through your heart must he walk – whoever wishes to go back,
for only you know that pathway – that fine, curved, effortless track.

(8 May 1955, afternoon)

Translated from the Bengali by Ketaki Kushari Dyson

Living on Hyphens

By Hugh Macpherson

KEKI N. DARUWALLA

Night River

Rupa and Co., Rs 95
ISBN 81 7167 480 1

KEKI N. DARUWALLA'S POEMS are fascinated and preoccupied by the shifting nature of things. They're much concerned with experience that's at transition point, at a quantum balance which could confirm or contradict itself – or may in the end still remain curiously ambiguous to us. The poems accordingly use a vocabulary of masks and dreams; of mirrors and pools that can reflect in different, changing ways; of shimmering islands; of hyphens held between possibilities; and of ferries that constantly shuttle between destinations.

Living on hyphens
a man needs to anchor himself.
Between dream and landscape
and between dream and the dark blood
congealing on cobblestones;
between hierarchy and disorder;
between the slow rhythms of seasons
and the frenetic pace of blood;
a man must arrive
at some sort of understanding.

('Living on Hyphens')

And:

Yet, how the mood oscillates.
Time, totally absorbed in its navel

as it is, is itself feeling uneasy
like a mare about to foal..

('Night River')

More light-hearted poems also enjoy the world's contradictions:

Live on the fringe, but die at the centre.
A good aphorism is one
which is true on the flip side as well.

Daruwalla includes in this collection a translation of a quatrain by the Urdu poet Faiz, who died in 1984. He includes two versions, with different emphases, different rhyme schemes, different atmospheres. Both have their own rival sense of conviction:

Night found your lost memories and swept them
in...

Unnoticed, the night brought your memories in...

Daruwalla was born into a Parsee family in Lahore in 1937, and has served in the police force in Uttar Pradesh and in the diplomatic service, including a posting to the Indian High Commission in London. He writes in English and published his first book of poems, *Under Orion*, in 1970. He won the Sahitya Akademi award in 1982 for *The Keeper of the Dead* and the Commonwealth Poetry Prize for Asia for *Landscapes* in 1987. *Night River*, according to my calculation, is his eighth collection. In Britain, his poems have appeared in *Poetry Review*, *Ambit* and *Acumen* and two were included in the recent anthology *Scanning the Century*. His poems have been translated into Swedish, Hungarian and Macedonian – at first sight, a rather random group of languages, but actually those whose speakers are amongst the most enthusiastic in Europe for poetry. He has read at the long-established annual Poetry Evenings at Struga in Macedonia.

Daruwalla writes about a wide range of places, and is fascinated by and carefully focused on them all. At times, it is true that he can almost sound blasé about this:

> Mostly when I arrive at places
> it is winter. Here it isn't...

But that touristic note is unusual. What is constant and impressive is a quiet, reflective voice which uses different contexts to try to get other perspectives on a central set of questions, to try to peer round the corners of contradictory experience by taking things from another angle, another country, or time of day, another mood or set of anxieties. Throughout this he is aware of and consoled by the beauty of the places he is has travelled to. Even when the situation is depressing and threatening he catches sight of:

> a lucky grove
> around a horse shoe pond,
> a humming bird
> that trembles like a cello.

The reader comes to share these preoccupations, and is drawn into them and the different ways they manifest themselves, looking out in company with the poet to learn more about how these aspects of life operate.

Islands are a recurring and rewarding theme in this and earlier books. In the 1987 'Landscapes' we encounter them in

> Morning: islands like somnambulists
> who had walked out on the mainland
> and awoke to find themselves
> waist-deep in the seas...

It's an economic and evocative way of getting us into a complex mood in four lines. In the new book there is an 'Island Poems' section about the Andamans, which opens with "A poem is an island in itself' and steers itself through surrounding seas to a convincing ending in which "in its own good time the poem peels off from the moment and the place".

These likewise are quiet poems, that don't scream "look at me and here I am and what about it", but stay with us, and are discovered there again in the morning, having waded out to some new position in our thinking where they've become familiar island shapes, silhouetted enigmatically across our mental horizons.

KEKI N. DARUWALLA
LUXOR DIARY

SMALL TRUTHS

Small truths need to be so small
that they are lost among larger things
which have no truck with truth.

Once the plague catches you
introductions become difficult.
You need royalty to usher you in;
never mind the place,
never mind the company.

When you go down
you need a pine-torch
you need an incense-burner.

When your son has embarked,
start your preparations –
wraps, jars –
and ask the lord of the hieroglyph
to be ready with his quill.

RAMESES III

They meet as equals always,
the Pharaoh and the gods.
Rameses has the boldness to slide
one arm round the waist of Isis,
goddess of magic and kindness,
healing and motherhood,
Isis in her glory, the moon-disc
caught between her horns.

Then he introduces his son
to the hereafter –
the hereafter with its own physics
and its own geology.
Meet the gatekeeper-god,
the dog-headed Thoth.
Meet Ptah, he says, the keeper of souls,
in a way the god of death.

Here too they are equals, except
he meets them with incense-burners,
while his young son, caught
by plague in Thebes,
carries a torch.

When its his own turn
to meet the mortuary gods,
Rameses knows he'll need them:
flame and pine-torch, incense
            and incense-burner.

THE IBIS-GOD

The ibis draws his lines
as he pecks at grain –
a string of dot and dash
that moves on the ground
in geometric perfection.
When the scribes saw this they said
"He is the lord of the written word,
and hence of learning!"
And where was learning more needed
than near the faultlines of the underworld?
And so Thoth, the Ibis-god
became the god of death.

FOOTNOTE

At the Luxor temple they met
the Nile-god and Rameses.
The papyrus of upper Egypt
and the lotus of the lower
are both yours now
            says the Nile-god Habie.

And beneath them a single rope
drawn across the necks
of a phalanx of slaves –
a Libyan from the desert,
a Nubian from the fifth cataract,
each dark and strong-thewed
and handsome as Rameses himself.

Under the celebration
the footnote of sorrow.

THE TEMPLE TO HATHOR

When you want peace
you send emissaries.
What Queen Hathshepsut sent
to the nation of Punt
were bead necklaces
and gold bracelets,
large enough to fit
the elephantiasis-stricken Queen
of that far land.
And the King of Punt, turbaned
and large-bellied and black
like some trader from a bazaar
in Madagascar, raised his hand
in blessing and peace, giving
panther skins and ivory in return.

But Hatshepsut had wanted
henna for her hair, and incense.
The King of Punt gave entire incense trees.
"Take them if you can carry them".
All this on the walls, painted
in oxidized colours.

There is drama on the walls as well,
a drama of erasures.
As incense urns are offered
to the gentle cow goddess, Hathor.
But where is Hathshepsut?
She's been wiped out.
The great Thutmose, who murdered her –
you are bound to be great if you murder
the only queen Egypt had before Cleopatra –
wanted her out of her own temple.

To preempt her reincarnation,
to make the hereafter itself short-lived,
a sure shot method was
to erase her from each fresco.
So Thutmose ravaged her tomb
and smashed the canopic jars

the rugs, though chiefly
they're interested in their own shadows.

It's an uneasy relationship –
shadows are in love with themselves,

and so are chairs.
The shadow teases the chair mercilessly –

You are here. No, you were here.
I can help you to be more.

No, help you to be less.
Sometimes they do seem to speak in unison,

both daring to interrupt the light.
The chair boasts of its personality.

The shadow is neither impressed
nor unimpressed.

Shadows are beyond all this.
Both know when something momentous

is happening – could it be
the soul of a chair has been repaired?

Has there been a change in the room's
slow, bright, geometric dance?

What are shadows made of?
Ghosts, or smoke?

They throw their sharp,
their tender nets –

and we are caught like fish.

Lost in Translation

By Ketaki Kushari Dyson

RABINDRANATH TAGORE

Song Offerings (*Gitanjali*)

translated and introduced by Joe Winter

Anvil Press Poetry, £9.95
ISBN 0-85646-311-6

THE BENGALI *GITANJALI* (1910), consisting of one hundred and fifty-seven lyric poems, most also given melodies by the poet-composer, is an important text in the Tagore canon. It is the first phase of a great lyrical surge that is contained in three collections: *Gitanjali* itself, *Gitimalya* (1914), and *Gitali* (1914). Though most of its pieces have their widest circulation as songs, Joe Winter is right to insist that "the poems are of importance regardless of their status as songs". The title *Gitanjali*, given to the English collection of one hundred and three prose poems, freely recreated, is somewhat misleading, as only fifty-three of them correspond to poems in the Bengali *Gitanjali*, and then in truncated forms. Because the English collection won the Nobel Prize, its name and Tagore's have become linked, though it is going over the top to claim (as has been done on the back cover of the present book) that this is the only volume of Tagore's poetry "whose name is known outside the subcontinent". Surely by now English-speaking readers should have picked up many other authentic names from the editions prepared by both William Radice and myself; besides, Argentines have long been familiar with the name of the collection Tagore dedicated to Victoria Ocampo: *Purabi* (1925).

Certainly, the Bengali *Gitanjali* deserved to be translated into English in its entirety. Winter, who aptly compares the English *Gitanjali* to "a sequence... of prayer-lamps" and the Bengali *Gitanjali* to "a deeply-illuminated festival of love", must be given credit for attempting to make that poetic *Diwali* accessible to a wider audience. However, he underplays the role of personal bereavements in the dynamics of this collection's spirituality, and he does not mention the possible influence of the Baul song-makers on that synthesis between religion and humanism that he rightly notices in the book. One small bibliographical error intrigues me. The date of the first publication of the English *Gitanjali* is given as 1913. That year the volume was awarded the Nobel Prize, but it had first been published in 1912. Considering that Winter's book was first published in Calcutta, I wonder how such an error could have crept unnoticed into the printed text. (I notice that he gets the first publication date of my edition of Tagore poems wrong by one year too: it should be 1991, not 1992.)

Winter set himself an ambitious target, to translate the poems into metrical structures, complete with rhymes. The results are uneven. Stanzas and lines impress with their felicity. Here and there whole poems pull it off. Good examples are nos. 22, 26, and 27, or no. 106, a historically-meditative, visionary poem with a pounding rhythm. But given the different habits of the two languages, sustaining the effort through one hundred and fifty-seven poems, without sacrificing meanings, was a Herculean task. Even in no. 106, the word *patita*, clearly meaning "outcaste", is translated as "you who fall" for the sake of rhyme. Bengali, with its abundance of words ending in vowels, facilitates fluidity and rhymes. Besides, the poetic conventions of the *Gitanjali* period permitted the mixing of literary and demotic linguistic forms, which enabled poets to juggle their syllables to fit line-lengths. This is a convenience we no longer have. Modernizing poets over the years have outlawed it; as Winter knows, Tagore himself abjured it in many of his later poems. Despite Winter's comments about the "belly-flop charade of the modern scene" in poetry everywhere, the reality is that every living language moves on, cannot stay put in one place, and the language of poetry moves on too; which is why translators have to adjust to the present state of their target languages, while the source texts recede – inevitably, inexorably.

Winter's effort to maintain metrical structures has caused areas of awkward padding, while his excessive dependence on words ending in -*ly* and -*ing* for rhymes has a tedious effect:

When in shame and undiscerning
blindness, from you I am turning –

you thunderously, as if through burning
    transform my black hell.

                   (no. 91)

The great original lines are scarcely recognizable.
Winter leans on *-ing* words even when the trick is
unnecessary, reducing the sonorous diversity of
rhymes in the original poems to a thin stream of
repetitive patterns. Poem no. 105 has seven rhymes
with *-ing* words in the first stanza, opening thus –

No more under this deadweight 'I'
is my head staying!
No more a beggar at his own door
for alms is praying!

– when he could have written, more simply, faith-
fully, forcefully:

I won't carry myself on my own head
      any more.
I won't be a beggar at my own door
      any more.

Odd uses of the English language in this volume
range from "let/my head kneel on the ground" (no.
1) to "still in kindness draw me/ your sacredness
toward" (no. 146). Can a head kneel? "Kneel" is
chain-linked to "knee": there are other suitable
verbs, surely. As for the inversion in the second
example, if Bengalis had perpetrated it, they would
have been lampooned for their quaint English.
Winter's English frequently sounds more archaic
than Tagore's Bengali of 1906-10.

I have noticed a crop of what could be called
"translation errors", but my main problem with the
Winter versions is that they often blunt the scythe-
like rhetoric of the original lines and fuzz up the
simplicity and clarity of the original images. Take
this example from no. 74:

Thunder sounds within your flute-song.
No light pastoral
sweet notes awaken: but to this
O make me sensible.

                 (no. 74)

The original is more like:

In your thunder plays a flute,
that's not a simple song!

To that tune would I stay awake,
give me the ears to hear it.

Winter's version of no. 121 opens as follows:

And so your joy has entered me –
and you yourself have come down too.
Without me, Lord of the three worlds,
this love of yours would be untrue.

Mais non! – as one might exclaim, what Tagore says
is more like:

Therefore you delight in me,
that is why you have come down –
without me, Lord of the three worlds,
your love would have been in vain.

Anxiety about form causes Winter's focus to
swerve repeatedly from the bull's-eye of poetry,
encouraging clutter and blinding him to simple,
feasible alternatives. What is literally "forget
precisely that" becomes, tortuously, "even let this
from your knowing vanish far" (no. 64). And what
is going on here? –

If with a sure care for life's state,
the flute is straight that I create –
then all of its air-openings
your melody will fill.

                 (no. 125)

Tagore is talking about making a simple musical
instrument out of one's life, more like:

If with my life carefully
I fashion a simple flute,
then surely with your own melodies
    all its holes you'd fill.

Winter's heroic venture confirms me in my
conviction that it is best not to have rigid pre-
conceptions about form when translating poetry. A
particular form should not be maintained if the
result is that meaningful statement gives place to
rigmarole. An adequate sonic pattern must indeed
be created in the target language, but each poem
may require slightly different engineering: we have
to play around with different aspects of language to
arrive at an acceptable structure. Overall, I feel that
Winter's current theoretical model simply could
not yield sustainable results over such a large corpus.

KETAKI KUSHARI DYSON
TOTALLY MULTICULTURAL

(With thanks to W. H. Auden)

Time will say nothing but I told you so,
Time only knows the price we have to pay;
If I could tell you I would let you know...

– W. H. Auden

"I am but ashes" – you say with a yogi's glow.
Listen, not only you, but I'll be ashes one day:
if I knew when, I would certainly let you know.

No matter what Ghalib says, the winds will blow.
Rough winds will shift you, scatter you straight away.
Will you remember that I told you so?

I could rub you all over me – for a tantric road show.
A mad yogini's role I would gladly play.
(But I'll need no pot to smoke – no, thank you, no!)

Or you could be the ash that makes my lily grow.
A ginger-lily, I would mark the air with my spray.
Imagine the fragrance, breathe in deep and slow.

But maybe your ashes do hide a fire's glow?
Are you not a flame burning in a lamp of clay?
If you have sparks to spare, will you please let me know?

Before you reap your ashes, your fire you must sow.
Your golden fire is the price you have to pay.
In a long slow fuse I'll sizzle, explode, and oh –
don't tell me later that I didn't tell you so!

Meta-reality for Hindus

By Shanta Acharya

The Best of Jayanta Mahapatra
Edited by P. P. Raveendran

Bodhi Books, 1995 (£7.95, Rs 145)
ISBN 81-7280-03 8-X

THIS LATEST SELECTION of poems by Jayanta Mahapatra is an admirable venture by the Bodhi Publishing House, part of a series of *The Best of Indian English Poetry*. The other poets included in this series are Kamala Das and Meena Alexander. The fact that there are no *Selected* or *Collected* poems of the major Indian poets is an indictment of the publishing world. While Indian writers of fiction are now well established in the western literary canon and some command high advances, Indian poets writing in English have been marginalised, both at home and abroad.

The general editor of this series, P. P. Raveendran (Reader in English at the School of Letters, Mahatma Gandhi University, Kottayam, Kerala), provides an introduction entitled: 'Decolonising Indian English Poetry'. The blurb points out that "any meaningful attempt at decolonising Indian English poetry can begin only by confronting the ideology of the aesthetic which historically was fashioned at the time of colonialist expansion in the Third World. The development of Jayanta Mahapatra's poetry over the past two-and-a-half decades is also the story of a gradual, yet firm, recognition of this need to confront the colonialist ideology". It is difficult to conclude whether such an introduction to any modern poet's work in India will do the poet any service in a post-modern, post-structural, post-colonial, post-every conceivable kind of ideological construct. The merit of literary criticism lies in its ability to direct the reader towards insights (Emily Dickinson would say "indirections") that s/he would not normally arrive at. It is true that certain ideological viewpoints are more suited than others, but as the editor himself points out: "Poetry now does something new not only to one's words, but to one's whole being. As Rushdie

suggested, Indian poetry now starts carving out large territories for itself within the English language, a fact which even the ex-coloniser, whether he likes it or not, is brought under increasing pressure to recognize".

In an article entitled 'Mystery as Mantra: Letter from Orissa' (in *World Literature Today*, Spring 1994) Mahapatra wrote: "My writing would go on to portray cultural values native to Orissa, not to other regions of India. And perhaps I have done just this in my poetry". The previous year, Mahapatra's first collection of poems written in Oriya, *Bali*, appeared. He has described himself as "an Oriya poet who incidentally writes in English" and suggested that his poems could easily be treated as "translations". For someone who has published some thirteen collections of poems in English and is widely recognised as a poet writing in English, such a self-portrait is revealing. Mahapatra is certainly not the first nor will he be the last poet/writer to be bilingual. Having been nurtured in the best of world literature available in English translations, planting himself Walt Whitman-like in Orissa (it would be very difficult today for writers to plant themselves in the Indian context without using the English language) seems a natural thing to do. In fact, it would never occur to anyone to suggest that he was ever portraying any other culture – Mahapatra has lived his entire life in Cuttack, Orissa.

It is only when one has cut through all these distractions and concentrates on the poetry itself that there is an opportunity to connect with his vision of life and universe as well as his use of words in getting there. In the first poem, 'Dawn', Mahapatra writes:

> There is a dawn which travels alone,
> without the effort of creation, without puzzle.
> It stands simply, framed in the door, white in the air:
> an Indian woman, piled up to her silences, waiting
>   for what the world will only let her do.

The Indian woman (not an Oriya woman) becomes just a woman in 'A Missing Person':

> In the darkened room
> a woman
> cannot find her reflection in the mirror
> waiting as usual
> at the edge of sleep
> In her hands she holds

the oil lamp
whose drunken yellow flames
know where her lonely body hides.

These themes are evolved memorably and with a sureness of touch in the two long poems included in this collection: 'Relationship' and 'Temple'. Raveendran provides an analysis of 'Temple'; critical appraisals do a much better job when they focus on the original text.

In the poet's notes to his poems, Mahapatra writes: "If the theme of 'Temple' is the plight of the Indian Woman, urged by the opening news item..., then there is reason to suspect little change, despite the seemingly dramatic changes depicted by today's media". The prologue refers to a news item in March 1980 which reported that the bodies of "an octogenarian couple" were found hanging in their house. The police believed they "committed suicide because of poverty and loneliness". The poem ends with another report in January 1986 that a 12 year old girl was "gang-raped and murdered". The police recovered her beheaded body, but no one had been arrested at the time of the report. The present format does not allow the reviewer to go into a detailed analysis of either these two powerful poems, nor the context of the *shakti* cult in Hinduism. "But to all accounts", according to the poet, "'Temple' represents a dream narrative; and perhaps Chelammal (the female protagonist of the poem) is a character in someone else's dream — unaware herself that she is a main figure in this dream, unaware too that this dream might restore her to the world of reality. It is difficult not to be influenced by the Indian doctrine of illusion, and I appear to have been taken in by it".

The poet describes a quintessentially Indian representation of reality which he defines as "meta-reality". In his notes, he writes: "The preconscious system of beliefs and values associated with the concepts of *moksha*, *dharma* and *karma* is a meta-reality for Hindus". The events reported in the newspapers are of universal significance and tragically continue to happen in most parts of the world. But, the poet's interpretation of reality has a unique Indian flavour which must be deciphered in order to gain full access to his poetry. It is perhaps no different than reading Eliot or Beckett without an appreciation of Christianity and Catholicism. The ability to live through uncertainties and empathise with "the other" spills through Mahapatra's words effortlessly, although he hedges his position by saying that "it is difficult for me to talk about the feminine principle".

JAYANTA MAHAPATRA
THE ROOM LIGHT

A familiar worn shirt hangs over the chair,
in this room where time retraces itself.
A wind from somewhere keeps struggling
with its empty sleeves, but one
rarely notices these things. Slowly
the world lying behind comes into focus.
It's like a film that goes on being neither good nor evil.
It's a country under the moon we failed to propitiate
where strange beasts called people
lie hidden in poor, unhealthy clumps of darkness.
Like the ones I once used to locate in crossword puzzles,

hidden in uncertain line drawings, but never
lost them again once I knew where they were.
But, now it's hard to believe what one sees.
The ones I find seem to beg to grant them
a reprieve from the earth. A pattern
that is afraid of those that make it:
the lifeless sky, the rust-red trains running
the same tracks day after day, the smell of anaesthesia
in hospital wards, the fear of loving
in whores lost between night and night,
the wet-greyed streets, and the bitten-down tears
that drag one unwillingly to the misery of Pasternak
and my own lost Kalinga War. And inside this pattern
I watch another face change and become my own.
Could pretense ever save one? My eyes, like these poems,
seek something to hold on to, hoping to steady
the hour. The old chair across the desk
is fallow with weariness; it begins to look around
like a survivor. Unopened places here, and the wind
that sounds the conch of some false dream.
Suddenly then, to see the room with its blank innocence,
to act as though I were another; and drifting
amid the frayed smells, I recollect
the fisherman I'd seen once on the sands,
the reek of fish about him, the dark strength,
the darker jungle,
the claw of time on his naked shoulder
I saw him brush aside lightly with his fingers.

TWO POEMS BY KHAN SINGH KUMAR
PACING THE CHANGE

"Mum always makes me cross my legs
and cover my head and pour milky chai
and Indian suits me for visitors
who sit in lines along our settees
to battle-ground the living room
by cross-firing stories of their old Asian days.

Meanwhile the girls from my class
are on their way to the High Street
and password whistle my bedroom –
I grab my black, Oasis bag
with its high heels and red lippy and other bits,
sneaking to the front door
                                        until
I'm stopped by my mother's endless mumbo-jumbo
(which they always hear and mimic) –
how in pride or sorrow our home lies
far in the mist of monsoons, how we must
soldier on until our work is done, how we
must all go home one day, only then will we
be released from this. Ms Victory,

my fave teacher, now she knows where I'm coming from:
she agreed with my diary entry about Romeo's banishment,
whispering how she could see it might be a travesty
but I must slow down to consider all the aspects.
She put her hand on my shoulder – ended
by joking in her rich English voice
which seemed so much a part of her:
Did the hare win the race?
And walked slowly, lugging a thousand smiles from me.

Sometimes I wish I was a black person too.
Black people are white people who got there before us.
Ms Victory has a white people's name.
Ms Victory goes clubbing
and comes back when she wants to.
I see her arm-chaired in front of the tele for a midnight feast.
She scoops up a spoon of trifle
and a howling of lovers are choking her phone line..."

TRENDY WOMAN BLUES

"Why now not be naked? You naughty western woman!
Not four month since I call you over and you're trolleying
newest Bombay passions to a choice
of ready made clothes. What confusion!
Never in my village had we changed our sweater,
Jesus Creeper, made of gold kohl pot.
We were proud of it. But this tightening of the bottoms
of the costume of the dowry of the sacred day
is drain-piping when we should be baggy
with a widening pride of the cardboard
at the base of the pyjama – a meeting of two
puffed curves into a perfect Punjabi smile –
what you have puckered into a bony ladies bellybutton!

Turn off those sunglasses. It is evening in winter.
Look at me – what is that cherry jelly
over the lash of your eyes? Are you bleeding upwards?
Those mascara scars? This half cut hair-mop?
Have I come to a skin-heading sex-change woman?

Even our peoples at the Sugar Puff factory,
I overhear the poison their wives at night monster
their crazy heads with: *She was in film star red* they say.
No, no, one says, *she's in chocolate sauce*, and another –
the blue boiler suit boy slaps his hands together,
choking, even louder says, *no, no, no,
I saw her at the broken biscuit stand
in the company of her Doctor, the Avon lady
and by all the Gods in my top pocket*, he says,
I swear she was in English poodle pink!
And they laugh and they toss up their chappatis
at the lunch time talk only of your toe nails.
I have to make up constipation for shame of leaving the loo!

You were the first educated, city wife in our family
and you abuse me for a Green Card.
How could you last night
tie my once 'B' team hockey body
with the jockstraps off the wall
(they were souvenirs from my College days)?
All night long – the beastly pouncing on my chest.

The tickling, the lipstick, the "odour toilet".
The neighbours of the terrace giggling. My father in a cough.
It was the worst waking from snores to screaming I ever make.
I can no longer meditate or pray or lock into my lotus position.
Even now, I can not close my legs!

O my Rub, what is England happening for us?"

Rub – God

SUJATA BHATT
BHAGAVATI

Bhagavati is one of the many names and forms of the Hindu goddess Kali.

On the train from Madurai
to Thiruvananthapuram – how I wait
for the flashes of red earth
          between the endless green
          of the coconut trees.

How I think of you, Bhagavati –

Here, the earth spills
          bright red from a gash
in a hill – there a field is slashed deep enough
for the red to show.

Where are you now?
Have you become
          the soul of one of these trees?
They say the Goddess lives here –
          could it also be you?

Look, everywhere the trees are turning
          greener, darker –
as if they want to hide in the thickening sky,
as if they too will shift to indigo.

I want to learn this all by heart,
I want to understand the shape of the light.

While the train rushes on faster
and faster – so there is a breeze,
so even the monsoon air
          turns a bit cooler.

But I would like to slow down
Bhagavati, I would stop this train
at least a hundred times between stations.

Bhagavati, how were you named?
Why did your mother
name you Bhagavati? You were born
and your mother thought "Bhagavati" –
Was it so simple? Perhaps she wanted you
to be strong, even fierce – you were already
beautiful – Perhaps she wanted the Goddess
to keep you safe –

You were sixteen-years-old
when they married you off to an older man
who took you to America –
How could your mother know
about the tumour
that would grow in your liver –
You were twenty-seven, maybe twenty-eight –
with three children: two boys and the youngest
a girl, barely a year old.
Who could imagine it was a tumour
that made you sick?
I remember chopping radishes
in your kitchen – fat red ones, so slippery
and so round – thinner and thinner
I chopped them – It was a game
to see how fast I could move the knife,
how thin I could make the slices, until the red
disappeared into slivers: wet threads of silk around
          the spicy white disks –

I was only fourteen then,
but I knew you didn't want more children –
knew how you begged to have your tubes tied.
          I knew you feared
your husband – how you protected your children

from him – In the end
you always spoke to my mother
on the telephone, when the children
were at school – yours and hers –
In the end the doctors cut the tumour out
from your liver – In the end that was all
they could do – In the end we visited you
in hospital and the first thing
you said was "good-bye".
In the end the doctors could not explain
what caused the tumour to grow – although
there were studies already
connecting the Pill to liver cancer – In the end
my mother was convinced it was the teflon, nonstick
coating on your pots and pans that got mixed
up with your food and poisoned your liver.
In the end you sent for your sister –
She was my age – and she hardly spoke to anyone.
Remember?
You were the age of my mother's sister
and I was the same age as yours – another circle –
                              remember?

In the end
you went back to Rajasthan
to die in your parents' home –

Bhagavati, the fields are full
          with young plantain leaves.
It is the brightest green I have seen in a long time –
Your daughter must be almost twenty-nine now –
They say the Goddess lives here –
But don't ask me why –
don't ask me why I think of you today
on my way to Kerala –
Don't ask me why
I like to repeat your name, Bhagavati.

ARVIND KRISHNA MEHROTRA
BHARATI BHAVAN LIBRARY, CHOWK, ALLAHABAD

A day in 1923.
The reading room is full.
In pin drop silence,
Accountants, homoeopaths,
Petty shopkeepers, students, clerks,
Turn the pages
Of the morning papers.
At the issuing desk,
Some are borrowing books:
A detective novel in Urdu
In two volumes;
A free translation
Of a poem by Goldsmith
Printed in Etawah,
Titled *Yogi Arthur*.

The books
Are still on the shelves,
Their pages brittle
And spines missing.
New readers occupy the chairs,
Turning the pages
Of the morning papers.
Turning pages too,
But of dusty records
In a back room,
Is a researcher from Cambridge, England.
It's her second visit,
And everyone here knows her.
She's looking at Indian reading habits
In the colonial period.

Outside,
On the pavement,
Is a thriving vegetable market.
Amidst the stalls,
A knife-grinder sets up
His portable establishment
And opens for business.

Survival

by Shanta Acharya

Chandrabhaga: A Magazine of Indian Writing

edited by Jayanta Mahapatra

New Series, Number 1, 2000
Tinkonia Bagicha, Cuttack 753 001, Orissa, India.
Annual Subscription Rates: Rs 150 (India);
Single copy Rs 75; Overseas rates US$25.

CHANDRABHAGA APPEARED TWICE a year for seven years between 1979–1985 but ceased publication in 1986. As Jayanta Mahapatra, its editor, reminds us: "In a world of changing social and technological values, whether a serious literary magazine with no fixed sources of financial support would survive once again is difficult to tell. We can only hope this would be possible". I second that hope and applaud Mahapatra's risk-taking under clearly difficult financial circumstances, and encourage the new *Chandrabhaga* to fare forward by attracting both good writing and funding.

The editor promises: "we hope to publish the best writing available to us, and to showcase the emerging and the established, especially in the realm of poetry". K. Satchidanandan's fine contribution of seven poems, originally written in Malayalam and translated into English by the poet and by A.J. Thomas, certainly deserve showcasing. The poem dedicated to his friend, who died of cancer, begins with: "Iron, glass, fire, water, / word: what material shall I / choose for your statue? / One rusts, another breaks, / others go out, dry up, fall silent, / nothing of man / remains". God is a theme that recurs in the Indian milieu. But Satchidanandan's poem, 'The Path Towards God', is worth re-reading:

"Attachment does not hinder / only practise it with detachment. / Love is way / if not confined to Man. / Poverty is divine / when not imposed".

In her 'Diary of Dreams', Meena Alexander deals with the nature of dreams and their betrayal, post-Pokhran. India has indeed come a long way from Gandhi's *satyagraha* to Pokhran, from a republic "fought for with prayers / burnt indigo, and steel" to "In Pokhran's desert / a bright bomb / caves soil / into feverish ruins". Living in the US now for several years, Meena Alexander knows a thing or two about dreams. Pijush Dhar's Five Pokhran Poems also emphasize "The morning sport that brings you fame / leaves the highway of love and leads / to a dark alley of bloody embrace". Dreams have a way of turning into nightmares and Yumlembam Ibomcha, a Manipuri poet, explores such themes skillfully. His poem, 'Story of a Dream', begins with the slaughter of the innocents, where "bodies of children lie about / like rats run over by vehicles" and goes on to add, surrealistically: "How happy I am being shot, / this bullet shooting into my mouth / is also a mellow grape". In his poem, 'Derived From a Puppy', he mocks conventional notions of heroism in India today, where life is cheap; and survival itself is a daily act of heroism.

Many of the poems deal with the double-edgedness of things, as Arun Kamal's poem 'This is the Time' ends with: "This is the time / when the old is gone / and the new is yet to come". The country itself is poised on the cusp of such metamorphosis. Kynpham Singh Nongkynrih's satirical comment on the visit of the Prime Minister to Shilong says it all: "And some say he came / homing in like a missile / and left flying like an arrow".

Unfortunately, the quality of the literary criticism included in this issue is not of the highest standard, although Pramod K. Nayar's piece on 'Poetry of the Nineties' does attempt to update our knowledge of recent Indian poetry. It is a commendable feature of the magazine that it gives the reader a glimpse of the range and power of Indian writing, not just in the realm of poetry which is its main strength, but also, for example, in a short-story such as 'The Clock', by P. Surendran, grippingly translated by Elzy Taramangalam.

Many of the poems are translations and, while the quality of the translations are uneven, sometimes within the same poem, Mahapatra gives us a wide selection of new writing flourishing in India today. Manoj Parida's poem, 'Drought', is the last poem in this issue. As *Chandrabhaga* is published in Cuttack, Orissa, where the cyclone in October 1999 caused unimaginable devastation, it is difficult to read this poem objectively, although the poem was written pre-October 1999. All creative artists make use of their suffering and misfortunes to retrieve some meaning out of it. I hope that in future issues Mahapatra will share with us the poetry of that shattering experience and the resilience of those who survive such events.

The Empire of Light

FRED D'AGUIAR FINDS A NEW SERENITY IN DEREK WALCOTT'S LATEST BOOK

DEREK WALCOTT

Tiepolo's Hound

Faber, £20

ISBN 0 571 20557 7

MIDDLE AGE APPEARS to force on poets the need to be expansive in their chosen medium. If poets contain Whitmanesque multitudes then their wish is to display all their wares at once, that is, in a long, discursive poem rather than in repeated takes over shorter poems. Derek Walcott first succumbed to this impulse nearly thirty years ago, aged forty-three, in his autobiographical poem *Another Life*. The poem is a rehearsal of everything he estimated himself to be up to that moment, leaning heavily on memory, both as a reliquary for the imagination and a repository of vision. *Another Life* is a love letter to youth and its strange morphing into memory but the poem also memorializes place. Island life, the seascape, tropical vegetation, perpetual summer, small-Island politics and inveterate poverty, all come under Walcott's scrutiny not as sociology but as properly linked to the poetics of place.

By the time he wrote his next long poem and perhaps his most accomplished, 'The Schooner *Flight*', he knew intimately the forces which shaped him – love of landscape, loss of a parent and past, and an intertwined Caribbean and English history feeding his mind. He learned fast how to deploy them all at once in the pressure cooker of the long poem, otherwise known as that extended riff on the soul, that marathon articulation of the undisciplined because splurge-like mass of the nervous and conscious systems. In 'The Schooner *Flight*', Walcott declares, "I've got Dutch, nigger and

English in me, / and either I'm nobody, or I'm a nation".

Walcott's 'The Spoiler's Return' is his next successful bid at the long-take poem, rather than the still photography of the truncated, though nonetheless prismatic lyric. 'The Spoiler's Return' continues Walcott's experiment with a Creole register side-by-side with standard English – this time in coalition with the satire associated with Pope but, actually, common to the calypso too. Spoiler, a deceased calypsonian returns to denounce the political corruption and social malaise that he sees all around in Trinidad. It is Walcott's most outwardly political tract and perhaps his funniest poem. Spoiler declares, "I decompose but I composing still".

His next long riff, *Omeros* (*Midsummer* is a hiatus, a sequence rather than a single entity) won Walcott the Nobel Prize and is his only best-seller (just one would do nicely thank you). But its alexandrines and chain-linked tercets tend towards humourlessness and earnestness, though never close to earning Craig Raine's unwarranted assault on it: "[in Derek Walcott's hands] Homer is coma". Homer is of course rather more accurately described as being on ecstasy in *Omeros*. Homer transmogrifies into Derek Walcott, probably the only other living poet besides Seamus Heaney to whom this process could apply.

Each book is a rehearsal of these set themes but from the viewpoint of a new variable – in *Tiepolo's Hound* it is nineteenth century Pissarro – as if its introduction plus the intervening years since the last examination of these themes by Walcott are meant to yield new insights. And they do. Maturity in years, time itself lashed to the temporal body, may well be the biggest variable of all in poetry. In Walcott it has resulted in a corresponding deepening of vision and aeration (for want of a better term) of expression – as he has become more profound in his thoughts he has managed to find apparently easier ways to formulate them: a heavy philosophy delivered in a lighter utterance. *Tiepolo's Hound* is the latest instalment in the long meditation that is both first and third person narrative and character-driven story. It is full of the wide sweep of fiction but lock, stock and several barrels invested too with the local delights of phrasing, image, rhyme and deep feeling usually associated with the lyric. The premise is simple, albeit in triplicate narrative form. First, Derek Walcott the young adult poet spots a painting of a hound at the Metropolitan Museum in New York. He thinks it is by Tiepolo or perhaps Veronese. It haunts him for thirty years. Second, he parallels this search for the hound with the life of Pissarro, a Sephardic Jew who left St Thomas for Paris in the middle of the nineteenth century to become a painter, only to find himself on the outside of Parisian salon life. Pissarro's struggle as a Jew and painter of the then new impressionist style parallels Walcott's struggle as a Methodist child in Catholic St Lucia and, on the larger canvas, his role of Caribbean poet in a Western European tradition. Third, he discusses recent European art history as a way to estimate his life-long obsession with water colour and to see the extent to which art can shed light (pun intended) on the life of the poet. In other words he tests the degree to which he can he borrow from painting in order to illuminate (in a reach for metaphor as clarity) what poets do in poems (or what poems do through poets).

In *Tiepolo's Hound* the couplet is the principle craft, iambic-driven, for the poem's forward propulsion. Couplets are wedded for added power – as if Walcott at seventy must drive a souped-up engine – in its infrequent ab ba and mostly ab ab rhyme scheme to the meditative length of the quatrain. The quatrain is Walcott's most natural bent – it is as if he breathes to the rhythm of four. The pitch of these lines is quite simply stunning in this book:

In that stroke of light that catches a hound's thigh,
the paint is all that counts, no guilt, no pardon,

no history, but the sense of narrative time
annihilated in the devotion of the acolyte,

undeniable as instinct, the brushstroke's rhyme
and page and canvas know one empire only: light.

The beauty of this utterance, a joy to say aloud, the feat of making it look easy, that is, no clutter in diction or syntax, belies the difficult ideas tackled here. Notions about painting, of how painting works on the senses before it seduces sense is perhaps the best analogy Walcott would have his reader make between painting and poetry. His vision is ultimately a-historical – the clear line, the clean brushstroke. Though heavily invested in history, in phenomena and in things, his poetry seeks to propel itself into a gravity-less space. He contemplates all things without clinging to any one thing. At the centre of *Tiepolo's Hound* is stillness of mind but without stasis of thought. Walcott's lines float in pure sound and sensation and concomitant sense.

My Muses pass, in their earth-rooted stride,
basket-balancing illiterate women, their load

an earthen vessel, its springs of joy inside,
pliant shadows striding down a mountain road.

In evening light a frangipani's antlers
darken over spume crests and become invisible

even to the full moon, and as dusk always does
for my eyes, and his lights bud on the black hill

to a cobbled brook's tireless recitation
in voluble pebbles as lucent as the ones

under the soles of the Baptist. Morning sun
on the corrugating stream over the clean stones.

The twenty beautifully reproduced paintings in the book reveal another side to the poet and playwright who said when he writes he hears actors talking. Clearly he must see them in a particular setting too. His eye for detail, especially landscape and colour, leaf, bark, and water and light is compelling, even if his figures are slightly wooden. He perhaps owes his highly textured and metaphorical language to this love of colour and light and their careful investigation as a painter. But from his youth where this metaphor and language tended towards the over ornate has come in this latest book a perfect command of their pitch and intensity. Seniority brings ease with his complex heritage: Caribbean material and a philosophic lightness equivalent to a state of Zen-like paradoxical heaviness of insight wedded to play and laughter.

Another Life

By Peter Forbes

BRUCE KING

Derek Walcott: A Caribbean Life

Oxford University Press, £30
ISBN 0 19 871131 X

PERHAPS LESS IS known about Derek Walcott than his major poetic contemporaries. Partly this is a matter of geography but even more it stems from Walcott's membership of that club whose journalistic sobriquet inspires such wrath in Michael Horovitz, the international super league. One always imagined him in boozy conclave with Heaney and Brodsky, enjoying a collective ethos that was necessarily exclusive. Such cliques can be a huge turn-off for everyone else. We had the work.

But Walcott has a huge *oeuvre,* a Nobel prize and can still divide critics – witness Craig Raine's recent demolition job in *Areté* – so a literary biography such as this might help us to focus a little better on his work.

The first impression is of Walcott's intense sense of vocation from an early age. If Andrew Motion aspired to be Poet Laureate, Walcott thought himself destined for the Nobel. He "knew before his teens that he was extremely talented with language and that he was meant to be a writer"; "His habits as a writer were formed early". Such dedication clearly can pay off but it also can lead to over-literariness, a self-defeating absorption in "literature" to the exclusion of literature's true subject. *Omeros,* his magnum opus clearly did his chances of the Nobel Prize no harm but many readers find it essentially static and a recapitulation of themes handled more freshly in his earlier work.

King is good on Walcott's career; how he earned his living; the milieu in which he operated at every stage of his life. He charts his emergence from St Lucia onto a world stage via countless readings, workshops, performances of his plays etc, even breaking down his income to show that by 1971"his finances were becoming dependent on the American market" – out of total earnings for the year of TT$21,500 only $2000 were earned in the West Indies. Although he did much to develop theatre and the arts generally in his island of St Lucia and throughout the West Indies, Walcott was always going to need a bigger stage.

Walcott had first gone to America in 1958, on a nine months Rockefeller Fellowship to study drama. But his crucial American roots were put down in 1963 when Robert Lowell was asked by Farrar Strauss and Giroux to report on Walcott's manuscript. So began a long friendship and a powerful influence on Walcott's poetry. From this point on Walcott belonged to the American literary establishment of the *New Yorker, Partisan Review,* and Farrar Strauss, as well as to the Caribbean.

America surfaced most strongly in Walcott's poetry in the 1982 book *The Fortunate Traveller.* With New England as the *mise en scène,* echoes of Lowell in the verse and a good deal of Hechtian American-abroad-in-European-culture subject matter the book was a kind of primer for the new internationalism: the "man from the margins" (Brodsky's phrase) repossessing the centre.

King is eloquent on Walcott's faults. He obviously holds him in the highest respect and there is no meanness in his verdict: at the beginning of Chapter 33 he enumerates Walcott's contradictions: high seriousness colliding with a love of scurrilous buffoonery; his juggling of several Caribbean identities: English, French, St Lucian; a constant striving towards clarity in poetry warring with a constant tendency towards over-elaborate metaphor. At times Walcott's ambitions have betrayed him, especially in his ill-fated collaboration with Paul Simon on the disastrous musical *The Capeman.* King says that Walcott was unduly in awe of Simon and the popular and financial success he had achieved. Even with a Nobel prize under his belt, Walcott couldn't resist the lure of a more demotic kind of fame.

Is it possible now to pinpoint Walcott's major achievements? The Creole of 'The Schooner *Flight*' has a more energetic movement than *Omeros* and 'Another Life' is perhaps the livelier epic. The *Midsummer* sonnets capture his dazed summer imagery perfectly, and then there are the individual shorter poems, 'Ruins of a Great House', 'Orient and Immortal Wheat'. Perhaps he has written too much and a *Selected* will be his passport to future readers?

Of revisionist assessments of a poet's worth there can never be an end – King's book is hardly likely to become definitive but it does shed light on a complex man.

FRED D'AGUIAR
RIDDLE

I am cull of the things single men
take for granted and married men
dream about, but only the young
at heart really own or can call theirs.

When prodded I curl up like a bud,
millipede or someone thrust into light
after days in a blindfold, or a fist.
And I don't open again, no matter

How long you wait and watch; and no
amount of coaxes and gentle strokes
helps. Do nothing and I am happy.
Say nothing to me and I sing all day.

You stepped over my grave yesterday.
You see my face but cannot name it.

Closer to Heartease

by Paula Burnett

LORNA GOODISON

Guinea Woman: New and Selected Poems

Carcanet, £6.95
ISBN 1 85754 486 2

"I WRITE WHAT I am", says Lorna Goodison. She writes as a woman, a black woman, a Jamaican, and not only a poet. Her parallel life as a painter is often evident in her poems:

My people are farmers
and artists

and sometimes the lines
blur
so a painting becomes a
december of sorrel
a carving heaps like a yam hill
or a song of redemption wings
like the petals of resurrection
lilies – all these require rain.

The specificity of Jamaica – its flora and fauna, its light and weather, the music of its speech – gives her words their distinctive savour. A phrase like "a december of sorrel", for instance, suggests a precise look and taste and a profound cultural meaning, as in Jamaica the Christmas season is celebrated by the home brewing of a sharp and sweet, clear, ruby drink from the fleshy red blooms of the sorrel plant

– not at all the same thing as British sorrel.

Does this mean, then, that the poems can only speak to other Jamaicans? No, it doesn't, as the composition of ideas and the music of the expression is strong enough to evoke a personal response. Readers will find themselves identifying with the situations addressed, although the parallels in their own lives may have different details. As she says, when her mother first objected to having what she saw as her private business made public in her daughter's poetry, Goodison reassured her by telling how people from all over said they recognised what she wrote as expressing their own stories, rather than hers or her family's. Derek Walcott, who praises Goodison's work for its "rooted, organic delight, true in its intonations to the Jamaican language she loves", long ago recognised the paradox that the more particular writing is, the more universal it becomes. These songs of praise, these elegies, are in a shared language.

Goodison, who in October took part in the *Poetry International* season on London's South Bank, has published three previous collections of poetry, *Tamarind Season*, *I Am Becoming My Mother* and *Heartease*, the second winning the Commonwealth Poetry Prize for the Americas region. Selections from these provide only a small section of *Guinea Woman*, however, which is largely new work. The tautness of the early poems may be missed. There is a longer-breathed conversational quietness to some of the recent work. Goodison has long had connections with North America, where she studied and has lived on and off, but she remains a Jamaican first. Although she now divides her time mostly between teaching at Indiana University, and her husband's Toronto, her poetic voice is rooted firmly in her personal history and the Caribbean's warmth.

Her skill is to take the ordinary and bring it out into that intensity of presence that hypnotises the eye just before the Caribbean twilight. A rare humanity breathes in her work, as she celebrates without sentimentality the distinctive graces of a way of life which is going now, "the overflowing bounty of my people's poverty". In a poem with a witty address to Wordsworth she recalls an illiterate great-grandmother who was "a poet / who wrote her lyrical ballads on air". There is often a sense of responsibility to the ancestors, recording the unrecorded glories of their lives. Listening to labourers joining in a worksong, she reminds us of the living African tradition in Jamaica, and recalls the "strength of Guinea women on our mother's side".

Yet there is also anguish, and a lively sense of the ways of the world. She bemoans the drugs culture that leads hopeful youths to prey on one another, and in a poem in which she calls like the good fairy for gifts for her son she includes injunctions to value books and earn good friends, but goes on wryly:

> but just to be sure,
> love books.
> When bindings fall apart
> they can be fixed
> you will find
> that is not always so
> with friendships.

Several poems mark formal rites of passage, saying farewell to a dead parent, greeting the birth of a child, and particularly, preparing food as an act of love. One poem serves up a recipe for the famous Caribbean dish, rice and peas, but it is simultaneously an eloquent celebration of her parents' loves and lives, a memorial, and a philosophy – a waiting for signs "that hearts are softening / that hard things are breaking open / that in the end it will all come together". Another sensuously defines poetry in terms of eating a mango.

Asked whether a vision of hope informs her work, she assents: "Yes, it would have to or I wouldn't bother to get up in the morning". Even when there seems every reason to give up in despair, she says, there's "always a larger vision at work in creation" and "you're evolving, you are moving, you're growing – you're going some place, no matter how it looks". The video recording from which this comes presents her in various Jamaican contexts, walking barefoot in the surf, sitting on a balcony against a green backdrop, a relaxed, generous woman with a fine smile and a heart-warming voice. 'Heartease', the title of her third collection, is where all of her work tends, in a questing and spiritual sense. She talks about natural cycles, about things going around: " you think you arrive at the same place, but you're really higher up on the spiral, reaching closer to heartease". That voice, and its comfort, is now more widely available.

In Search of the Ironic Republic

By David Kennedy

KWAME DAWES

Midland

Ohio University Press, $12.95
ISBN 0821413562

IN HIS NOBEL Lecture *The Antilles: Fragments of Epic Memory*, Derek Walcott refers to "the ironic republic that is poetry". In a Caribbean context, the irony stems from the fact that St-John Perse, the Guadaloupe-born child of French plantation owners, was the first writer, Walcott asserts, to capture the feeling of local life. A similar sense of irony and the influence of Walcott pervade *Midland*. The book's opening sequence is dedicated to him. More to the point, the title *Midland* evokes the older poet's *Midsummer* and Dawes's work is full of passages that would not be out of place in many of that book's fifty or so poems:

> At midmorning, we watch the green of tobacco stanzas,
> such even reckoning of this state where a nation
> carved its name
> into Cherokee country...

> ('Blues on Highway Fifteen with Krystal')

This shares so much with Walcott as to be virtually indistinguishable from him. There is the same careful relation of speech and metre which gives the sense of listening to a highly literate conversationalist. There is the detached, slightly self-regarding elegance and the striking self-reflexive opening immediately undercut by an awareness of politics and of the literal physical impact of imperialism. The irony here is that poetry's ability to register sensuous apprehension and equally sensuous self-consciousness mean that it is equally alert to the realities underlying them.

Walcott is not the only older writer present in *Midland*. 'Holy Dub', 'Map Maker', 'Excursion to Port Royal' and 'Epoch' have epigraphs from Kamau Brathwaite, Wilson Harris, Ishmael Reed and Ralph Ellison. In this context, the very differ-ent self-consciousness of 'Liminal' is at the heart of the collection:

> I should have been born in the epoch of flesh
> mongering...
> But I've arrived in this other time...
> I am gathering the relics of a broken threnody,
> lisping psalms – all I have – and crying salt and
> wet.

Midland's blurb quotes Eavan Boland on the book's "painful and vivid theme of homelessness" but it seems to me that this homelessness is as much artistic as literal. The older writers Dawes invokes can be said to have brought particular voices, idioms and experiences to their first articulation and to have begun the vast process of counter-narrative which Salman Rushdie has memorably termed "writing back to the centre". Throughout *Midland* there is a powerful sense of finding oneself dispossessed of an inheritance of dispossession. This is clearly articulated in 'Parasite' which begins by talking of "feasting on the dead with their thick scent of history" and concludes:

> I hear myself turning
> heir to the generation that understood the smell
> of burning flesh, the grammar of a stare, the flies
> of the dead, undisturbed in an open field. My burden
> is far easier, it's true. I have not acquired a taste for
> chitlins
> and grits, but I wear well the livery of ageless anger
> and quiet
> resolve like the chameleon of suffering I am.

Midland, then, expresses an awareness of having a debt to history and a corresponding sense of being detached from its narratives. However, if Dawes is often uncomfortable about what to write, I am equally uncomfortable with how he writes it. I began by drawing attention to the influence of Derek Walcott and I finished *Midland* feeling that Dawes had been overpowered by him. His tone, rhythms and rhetoric are everywhere. Phrases like "the iambic ebb and roll of the sea" and "women's slippery parts in the smell and shape of the island" are, like "tobacco stanzas", *echt* Walcott. Influences aside, Dawes has a tendency to shade into cliché – "alien shore", "elaborate conceits" – and into windy rhetoric – "the epic cataclysm of fire", "the psychotic lament of Wagner". The blurb describes Dawes as "a world poet" and, in the context of Walcott's influence and Dawes's own lapses, this suggests that *Midland* is a particular kind of poetic commodity which Western culture finds highly desirable. For "world poetry" describes a "writing back to the centre" that doesn't give the centre too much trouble. It says that, in Walcott's words,

"language is a place of struggle" or gives uncomfortable reminders about empire days but does so in an easily consumable form. The centre remains undisturbed by any whiff of the combative or the perfomative. It would be hard to imagine Brathwaite being termed a "world poet". Which suggests that the greatest irony of poetry's republic is that it isn't one.

The Road to Freedom

by Graeme Wright

FRED D'AGUIAR
Bloodlines
Chatto & Windus, £12.99
ISBN 0 701 16958 3

Mangan

"WE CANNOT ESCAPE history". Thus wrote Abraham Lincoln in 1862 when his country was being torn apart in a Civil War which divided families over the question of slavery and its economic implications. The same quote could justifiably serve as an epigraph for Fred d'Aguiar's remarkable novel-in-verse.

Taking as its central theme the fated affair between Christy, the white son of a plantation owner and Faith, a black slave, *Bloodlines* leads us through a labyrinth of prejudice and social dogma from which we have never been able to shake ourselves free. Narrated for the most part by Faith and Christy's son, the book also looks at attitudes to mixed marriage and mixed blood in a compassionate and thought-provoking exploration. Readers of Byron will be familiar with the ottava rima pattern from *Beppo* and *Don Juan* which d'Aguiar manipulates like a sculptor to mould his story. It has been argued that the first canto of *Don Juan* is consciously autobiographical; in roaming

the cul-de-sacs of the slave trade d'Aguiar presents us with a work which is consciously ancestral. Voices of resentment and confinement, of lassitude and persecution echo through its stanzas like the ghosts of slaves – d'Aguiar here follows two of his influences, Bob Marley and Linton Kwesi Johnson who have both written expansively and passionately on similar subjects.

Faith and Christy's escape from the plantation, the depth of their love and the ultimate futility of their affair form a furiously paced opening to the book. When Christy is captured and sold to a travelling show as a prize fighter we gain a valuable insight into white man as slave, man as entertainment fodder and his subsequent disposable "value":

Christy faced a black oppo
    nent twice
his size and did not know
    what to do.
At first he took punches,
    ducked and sliced
air around the man's
    temples with a few
reserved swings aimed at
    white space,
until the man spoke. I'll be lynched if you
let me win. His red-rimmed eyes pleading.
Christy nodded and launched his farewell greeting

The narrator, having witnessed his own birth and Faith's death in the process, is brought up by a white couple, the Masons, who despite their liberalism never forgive him for being a half caste and resent him taking their surname –

"You don't know who you are because, young
    man, you're nobody, neither black nor white!"

The Mr. Masons of middle America prospered
in the enlightened aftermath of the Civil War.
Slavery may have been (all but) abolished and yet
blacks and mulattos were regarded as second class
citizens for at least the next hundred years. There is
an aptness then that the narrator is cursed to
immortality until the races become equal:

So history greeted me. I am condemned
to live an eternity, unless all the conditions
that brought me into being somehow mend:
I mean Slavery and all its ramifications
marching unfazed into the new millennium.
Everything that I see in countries and nations
tells me this is true: Slavery may be buried,
but it's not dead, its offspring, Racism, still breeds.

Bloodlines is, above all else, a book of nightmares
and dreams: nightmares of war and slavery, of a lost
Africa and its homeless people, of torture and incar-
ceration. The dreams are of freedom and peace,
Africa and America united, of fusion and acceptance. Balancing these nightmares and dreams is
the key to d'Aguiar's success and, as he did with his
novel, *The Longest Memory*, he retreads the road
which threads through man's inhumanity to man
with a sureness of step and resolution. Only towards
the end of *Bloodlines*, with the narrator arriving at a
new century of freedom and equality does d'Aguiar
exercise his other skill, that of dry humour –

This train I'm on's really bound for glory.
This train – going by the light seeping in –
is nothing if not extremely holey.
Hallelujah! This is not a gravy train.
That's something poetry can never be.
Though it can bring with it a little fame.
My train is death but the engine is my craft.
Death wins but poetry gets the last laugh.

Bloodlines, as the inside cover advises, should be
read fast like a novel. And then, in this reader's experience, reread slowly to savour d'Aguiar's language
to the full. Only then will its message ring out loud
and clear.

E A MARKHAM
TWO MEN AT THE CASSAVA MILL

It's here in the front yard near the water-trough,
well clear of the grass where Nellie spreads
her sheets, starched white with *blu*, to dry;
two men, one in short pants, working in tandem
grinding cassava enough to kill the village.

It's a *coffin*: the woman looking down from the verandah
at ground cassava shrouding its box, under the mill,
will not give in to the fear prickling her
to leave this place *soon* with her son, still in short pants:
she shuts her eyes not to see the men in action:

Left foot on a board, on the ground, stable.
Right foot peddling, pressing down on the pole,
easing up on the pole – boy hugging man –
up and down in tune with the man who feeds peeled cassava
into the throat of the wheel. He is expert

and won't soil cassava-snow piling up underneath
with gratings from his fingers.
The man has no thoughts, he is dumb.
This is the 1950s, no one will know what he thinks.
The mother will shut her eyes at this ritual of men

intimate in public. The best she can do
is freeze the boy permanently behind
this rough man from the village: *why do they work
so well together?* The boy will change from short pants,
label the suitcases, and head for England with a grudge:

he will always be second-carpenter in this scene.
No one will recognize the force of his stubbornness
Grinding the cassava grinding the cassava
behind this dumb man in protecting the village
from disaster. For the mother is reduced

to panic, and the man in front is trapped
in *folk* memory where no *sign* translates him into language,
and anything you like *You're the woman of my dreams woman
of my dreams Rampant and foul-mouthed, endless
in America, etc.* can be put into his mouth.

I'm writing this on a computer in England,
a boy grown out of suits, years past burying
the mother. And the man grinding the cassava
is of course dead, the village new-poisoned by ash. A volcano,
this time. And who wants, anyway, to grind cassava at a mill!

I'm writing this on a computer in England
remote from the house, no mango at the back, no grape-
vine facing the edge of Mrs. Meade's land: this
could have happened anywhere; the cassava smell has gone,
and nothing colours the evening air with home

but a vast night that prevents you sleeping.
And I sense what the dumb man might have thought,
and console myself. And I indulge the image of a mother protecting
her son. Yes yes, you say: but what's this got to do
with the price of coffee in Brazil. Or murder in Kosovo?

RAFAEL ALBERTI
THE RETURNING OF A RAINY AFTERNOON

It must be raining now as well, misting
In those bays of my deaths,
Of my years still alive without deaths.
Raining, too, in the pine grove mist,
And storming as well, the now distant
Rolls of thunder feted with cries, the final thundering,
The last lash of lightning in the towers.
You would lean out, white old age, emerging
From your warm sheets of grandchildren and gentle eyes,
And my mother stood at the stained-glass windows
Of the high mirador that revealed
A blue city of snowy shadows
With green railings
Ringing suddenly to afternoon
From fingers the sea secretly,
As if carelessly, abandoned in the breeze.

I'd go off with Agustín, with José Ignacio
And Paquillo, the coachman's son,
To hunt for snails on adobe walls
And among hedge mustards of tombs,
Or in the broom-thick lost grove,
To cape calves still feeling frights
Of joyful schoolboys suddenly surprised.
(These lost gusts unexpectedly returning,
These rushing words from woodlands,
An interrupted dialogue, secrets
Of sea and soaking sands.)
I bow my head,
Put my ear in the hollow of my hand
To go over better what comes surging
Back to me from far away, with the waves of there,
With those from way off. I hear a gallop
Tiring the coastline of castles,
Of bathed ruins and stairways
With their feet destroyed in water.
I know who's there, who races off
Singing on that black colt of salt and spume.
Where's he running to,
To what underwater doors, what thresholds

Of moving blue, to what clear interiors,
In search of a profile, a compact
Form, line, colour, relief, music
Tangible and defined?
He wants the arches, looks for the lintels
Leading to difficult towns without mists,
Harmonic regions, precise firmaments,
Skies without nebulas,
Smokeless paradises.

It's raining without sea, with no sea at all. It's
Been erased by the brume. Soon
It'll take the woodlands too, and not even these trunks,
So possible and easy,
Will sway on foot to tell me
They've died, as have
My eyes this afternoon of mists and rain.
Who sees in the dark,
Yearns for shadows,
Who'd lend substance to the starless night?
The sea died, as did
The things that arrived with it. There only
Remains, only, you hear?,
A confused conversation, a rambling
Discussion without words to grasp, a feared,
Invading terror
Of going back without eyes, of shutting them without sleep.

Translated from the Spanish by Louis Bourne, from Retornos de lo vivo lejano,
'The Coming Back of Distant Life', 1952

TANURE OJAIDE
OLOYA

I

I seek you through labyrinths of learning fields
to sharpen my ears and tongue with resonance

for who has sung well or heard melodies
without listening to your ringing voice?

I listen to singers of the mapped world
and find no voice that matches yours

that in your day made singers bow and
give way at the sight of you in the arena.

I too sing and, learning, want to imbibe
the special flavour of your tongue.

I put aside the basket of abuse
to spray you flowers of adoration –

you have captured a crowd of devotees
& I fall into the song-inducing trance.

II

Oloya Oloya Oloya

I have come to draw from your deep-hidden well
draughts fed by miracle undercurrents,
and now sit by your song-stoked hearth

to partake of the communion of songs
& learn how words leap to life
in the flavouring tongue of the master.

You garnered from the fugitive tribe of words
a treasure trove of self-patented songs
that rise above known melodies.

Through your lips restive with passion,
thought and feeling transformed into singing birds
whose colours and notes captured the world.

You captured the market spilling over town,
you captured the united nations of peers,
you even captured the ears of gods hard of hearing

with the sheer resonance of known words.
There was none who heard and did not
respond to the trenchant call of your tongue.

When you opened your mouth,
the keeper of words lacked restraint
& with left and right gave you the choicest.

Aridon raised you to the sky,
your evergreen foliage crowned every height
& the world became your glued spectator.

I come to you to know more of the trade –
teach the kneeling devotee your secrets,
place your palm on my advancing forehead

& let me carry the burden of black clouds
that will explode into glistening beads of words
and run a full-throated river of songs.

III

It's not the length of the trumpet that counts
but the full heart and breath of the blower

So many trees of truculent trunks in the forest
but we pass them by to worship the *iroko*

In the quest for beauty every aesthete arrives at yours
and collapses on knees to chant your praisename.

After you have reached the river the thirst disappears,
after a flurry of thunderstorms drought hides its wilting face

You rolled barrels of words over violators of communal codes,
you were the people's shield and spear in battle.

You stand taller than Arhuaran in our memory,
song-master with the tongue of divining words

your songs are the leaves of the fortune tree
& nobody sets out to count them

for in the black anthill that commands attention
the grains of soil multiply into your repertoire.

You conjured words from everywhere and nowhere,
dressed and deployed them to silence loud-mouthed rivals

they reached their target and unleashed their power –
the parrot-crew never failed to land across mountains!

But *Owena* of words, if I consider the length of the snake
I'll not find a long enough stick to strike it.

It's not the duration of service that tells the power of a god,
I devote these moments of the festival season to you.

Every song must come to a pause, if not stop
& for now I place near-hand my ivory trumpet.

The world ululates for the bride
& we install the king of songs to serve with songs.

(Lagos, August 8-10, 1999)

MARC TRITSMANS
OLD PEOPLE'S HOME

He draws the self same floor plans
from morning to night. That was
the house they lived in. Not a square yard
must ever be removed.

She is back to essentials: rocking,
humming, muttering nursery words, powdering
the tender, plastic buttocks of a long lost
son. They only meet each other

when, in a shared bed, as though by chance,
old hands happen to touch, lives
intertwine. Grant that at one such moment
they reach the end together.

Translated from the Dutch by James Brockway

MARK HALLIDAY
LIVIN' IN THE WORLD

I'm livin' in the world. I said I'm livin' in the world.
My shirt is sweaty from the filmy hot sun
and I'm livin' in that. Yeah I'm livin' inside of that.

I got my old black shoes. You know the leather has creases.
I got my pale old face with some freckles, mm-hmmm
you know it's got some creases.
Baby baby I'm creased.
I keep on livin' in the world.

You think I'm not a big deal. Yeah well that's your point of view.
And you're livin' in that.
Oh I'm sure you got your own troubles;
sure, cuz baby look where you live:
I mean you're livin in the world –
or so I have to assume! I mean I should be assumin'
that you are very human

but like, that's not my focus.
I said that's not what is my focus.
My head is full of my livin', sweaty heap of old livin'
in the self shop, mmm-hmmm,
I'm workin' long hours in the self shop.

I'm walkin' Forty-Third and Locust.
You know my laundry's not done.
You know my novel's not done.
It's called *Livin' in the World*.
Every chapter is a cesspool!
And I'm a purple submarine.
You think you know what I mean.
But you don't care all that much.
You've got your spouse and house and such…
Okay, go think about them.
But I am livin' in the world.

Yeah, my car's engine sounds bad. It kind of smells like burnt toast.
Was made in 1985. It wants to give up the ghost.
But at least I have a car; I can drive into town.
Maybe stop at the bakery – get me some sourdough bread.

Or maybe some ruggulahs.
I do like ruggulahs. Oh you don't care what I like!
So then I come out of the bake shop,
I've got a parking ticket. Because I'm livin' in the world.

I said I'm livin' in the world.
It's just an all-day buzz.
It is that in which I focus,
walkin' Forty-Third and Locust.

Well, you can take away my job.
You can say I have a shallow grasp of postmodern pluralism.
You can say I fail to excavate
the privilege encoded in the speech of my class.
In the speech of my social class, mmm-hmmm.
Yeah I got this privilege: it doesn't always feel so great,
it's like a shirt that's slightly itchy
but it fits into your theory.
That's how you might live in the world, you might have
a theory. Okay, go think about that.

Oh the sun is blurry hot upon Locust Street.
And I'm inside my sweaty shirt.
I got my narrow hungry buzzin' little life
and I am livin' in that.

You know I've done some stupid things –
hey I could give you a list;
I've done some chickenshit things.
Oh the list could get long.
But I am livin' in the world:
in my sweaty old Kansas City Royals shirt!
Yeah my Kansas City Royals shirt!
I don't see my other choice now.
I keep on livin' in the world.

HARRY CLIFTON

A VISION OF HOKKAIDO IN THE RAIN

*A Japanese Christian sect believes Christ visited the country
in his unrecorded years*

It is very quiet here, in the north of Japan,
Where everyone has forsaken me. The street
Is rain-black, drizzled, and it seems to be winter,
Probably late at night. My second coming,

Unannounced, past any civilised hour,
Is still too soon for redemption. Dark before dawn –
The market closed, the basins for live eels
Stacked neatly. One old woman in black

Squatting under the light of a low-watt bulb
Spoons noodles into herself. Do the old, I wonder,
Go as they always did here – to the boneyard
Deep in the mountains, in the inhuman cold,

And die back into their lines of ancestry?
Laughter behind closed doors, through the masking tape
Of broken, bandaged windows, in the geisha parlour –
Canned American laughter on TV.

Perhaps they are sleeping, though, the guiltless women,
With their clients gone, oblivious on *sake*,
Screen still running. Slide them back, the panels –
Earthly paradise! I have foreshadowed it all,

Of course, from the other side of time
Now here I am. A *tuk-tuk* through the small hours
Sheds its wake of sparks in the neighbouring street
(If everyone were suddenly to awaken...)

And the elephants, asleep in chains
Outside the sawmill, dream of time and motion
Hauling logs. Miasma of cured hides –
So this is a town that lives off tannery, then,

And entertains itself, like a million others,
Eating, having sex and watching soaps.

And to speak of evil, as the rain drifts down
Past the naked bulbs of the marketplace

Left on all night, is to know redundancy
Under another wisdom, a different kind of law
Than the one that brought me north, so long ago,
In my lost, apocryphal years

Between the carpenter's shop and the death on the cross.
Perhaps no more was needed. Had I stayed
And intermarried, God alone would have known
And everyone could have slept to the end of time.

VONA GROARKE
POP

It's all love and loss and what was never said
these days, when our radio's jammed between stations
and we oscillate from talk of war to organ fugues
and a spray of pop thrown over night-time hours.
We ghost events, significance and sound, and want
to think this better than a silence we've compiled.

As last week the headset of my Walkman buckled
just as the voice inside aspired to new heights
it never would scale now. So Dusty never
made it to the French bits, and those words
(ne me quittez pas) were beached on the other
side of some vague silence, glittering and pristine.

Where they were useful, maybe, to those whose work
it is to gather in our unstruck notes and words
we never spoke when there was time and breath
to let them go. Whatever had been on the tip
of the tongue, that never slipped; a misremembered
name; a choked-back curse; a promise never made;

unruffled grace notes; misplaced tunes, and all the
unwritten songs about being young that never got us
anywhere. Like the one I love but can't remember,
getting the words in the chorus all mixed up.
I know it isn't "live" although I sing it. It's "leave".
And it's really not "forever". No, it's "over".

NIGEL FERRIER COLLINS
WHINGE

I saw the worst poseurs of my generation fastened on the tit of Nanny State,
    glutted histrionic autolatrous,
flouncing their personas through gentrified bohemia looking for
    an uncritical sponsor,
ego driven chancers ligging for lucrative connection
    to the heart of gullible throwaway society,
who designer scruffy shifty-eyed and hyped boogied all night
    in the ultra blue of condominia air guitaring
    across the roofs of suburbia to lager lout garage bands,
who marketed their perpetual adolescence in plate glass colleges
    reverse-engineering reputations as mid Atlantic Beats
collaging, plagiarising, doodling tripsical whimsicalities
    dribbling scribbling and just plain leaving it blank
    too laid back to do more than sign and price it,
who were not content to write but had to BE poets with nods to Blake
    and Villon and random outbursts of aischrolgia and gratuitous use of
    obscure language cross referencing their mutual admiration so
    comprehensively they kept parasitic academics in a frenzy of
    annotation for decades,
who cultivated madness put their heads in electric ovens overdosed on
    aconite grazed their wrists jumped in front of invalid cars and hung
    themselves from baby bouncers,
who giggly on dope sashayed out from squats into middle earth or the park
    on missions to find long lost stashes under Angel Bridge,
who turned on, tuned in and stayed there for years with somapsychotic
    dependence on equally confused local shrinks,
who sat in the square laughing chanting at ghosts and passers-by
    forcing eructations from quasi aboriginal instruments,
who frightened themselves in their crash-pads and scurried back to mummy
    Christ or got abducted by aliens,
who became depressed and found God and donated everything they owned
    whole families in thrall to megalomaniac self-made prophet
    paedophiles,
who came out as divan divas lederwolves cling film buffs pony-girls enema
    agents shock absorbers depilated adamites immerdants cottagers
    frottagistes,
who missed the fun and became social workers fantasising about satanic
    abuse breaking up families parents everywhere too scared to touch
    their children,
who friendless and bitter and hysterical stabbed nurses and battered truck

drivers to defend the rights of foetuses and sheep,
the most pampered and protected generation in history marching to reclaim
    their right to be angry,
who primal screamed rebirthed regressed to derivative episodes from former
    lives,
who were tucked and plucked and liposucked in magic time reversal rituals
    which failed year after year after year,
who lost themselves in a continuous nostalgia roadshow grubbing up
    empire detritus and rusticana to make-over their converted oast
    houses,
who lobbied for mediaeval punishments for violent crime and swung wheel-
    wrenches at strangers in road rage incidents,
who fawned over Tibetan villages, Native American rituals, African
    nomadic customs but were too xenophobic to welcome local
    minorities,
who packaged themselves to the poorest nations on earth in search of
    quaint destitution and child prostitutes,
who were disloyal lazy careless rude aggressive dangerous absent and sacked
    and took employers to court for unfair discrimination,
who date-raped their way from Bristol to Glasgow with Rohypnol and lies
    unloving unloved unlearning unfulfilled and rich from chart topping
    raps,
who rejected the system and disappeared into the sodden dereliction
    of Celtic fringelands rolling their own in leaky caravans hovels tipis
    eking out a living on benefit frauds and seasonal drudgery,
who raised litters of inbred cats and bedraggled children who later became
    teenage parents of ever more dispossessed children ripping each other
    off and slowly gathering anger as the system transforms itself without
    them,
who took to the road in decommissioned buses with mangy dogs begging
    pilfering cursing their way from cold water camp to camp crescendo
    of demanding,
who bedevilled festivals selling bent cutlery, friendship bands, vegan
    footwear shapeless remnant skirts primary school crafts soaked in
    patchouli,
who finally admitted they were junkies and had their demons cast out by
    manic evangelists all night vomiting and gibbering in tongues,
who prattled in lantern land steeped in scrying graphology necromancy
    anthroposophy aromatherapy Feng Shui Hopi ear candle
    treatments crystal healing postal Tarot remote healing,
who were drawn to any cryptomantic phenomena crop circles UFOs lost
    tribes teleportation homeopathy Roswelliana Kirlian photography
    alien big cats,

who were prey to hoaxes publicity stunts coincidences Chinese whispers
new age capitalism hallucination mass hysteria paranoia and pre-
senile dementia.

STEPHANOS PAPADOPOULOS
THE HUDSON RIVER

For Andrew M. Vickery

On days when the wind, like stubbled sky
over the Hudson, creaks on a rusty hinge,
mulls a blankness, a vacuumed space
where the thought shrinks like a slug in a tin
of saltwater. On days like this it's better
to sleep, or mouth some pre-Socratic phrase
till the bleakness becomes second nature,
till words like βιος μακρυς[1] melt
like cotton candy on your existential tongue.

I go out for a walk along the river.
Over there, New Jersey awaits its renaissance.
A glance at open water is salvation,
and the birds, whatever your temper,
can always be watched, their splintered flight
over the stumps of a long lost pier,
like a sheaf of papers thrown to the wind.
I'd rather not take up the pen today –
what would I write other than the days
are getting longer and the month changes name?

I am used to small redemption, a smile
on a street corner leading to open vistas –
but some days sink mercury-like, closing
the distance an eye can travel, winching your gut
with the inching crank of Archimedes' screw.
Out on the Hudson the Weehawken ferry struggles
against the full tilt of a north wind.
Sloppy waves batter the awkward tin tub's hull,
seagulls spinning like ashes over the wake
as it chugs its redundant journey
from riverbank to riverbank and back.
On days like this my mind repeats the pattern,
like the needle howling against the blank edge

[1] Long life "life is long" (Ancient Greek)

of the phonograph, it lurches against itself
The river, a cut vein, drains
into a vast blue where distant tankers
float on a thin horizon, and the eye
can rest, if only for a moment. Nothing
widens like this emptiness over which we pass –
a light, expendable traffic.

W.D. JACKSON
RILKE: THE CAROUSEL

Rotating in the shade of its bright roof,
For a little while this gaily coloured stand
Of horses from the slowly vanishing land
Of childhood moves, though they don't move a hoof.
Though some are hitched to coaches, they don't pant;
But all of them have brave and eager faces.
A fierce red lion puts them through their paces,
And now and then a pure white elephant.

As if through trees, a stag swings into view,
Wearing a bridle, reins and saddle, where
A little girl is buckled, dressed in blue.

And, on the lion, a boy – not yet a youth –
Rides white and holding tight with one small hand.
The lion itself exhibits tongue and tooth.

And now and then a pure white elephant.

And, on their horses, riding through the air
They come; and fair-haired girls who – if the truth
Were told – are too mature for such uncouth
Horse-jumping, looking here, there, anywhere –

And now and then a pure white elephant.

And so it hurries past to its conclusion,
And whirls and circles on without an aim.
Reds, greens and greys in colourful profusion;
A profile, hardly worthy of the name;
Sometimes a smile, as if in sweet collusion,
Still dazzling – blessed – and wasted on the illusion
Of this blind, breathless game...

JOHN WHITWORTH
LOVELY CRICKET

*Avid listeners will know that Johnners and Trevor and Fred for different reasons
are no longer with us alas.*

There's Aggers and Blaggers and Johnners and Blowers,
There's Fred and old Trevor (who's awfully clever),
There's the Beard and the Nose and a cake from Dundee
Baked by Mary MacPherson (or some other person)
And Zimbabwe are 7 for 3.

They're 7 for 3 and they're following on.
But the covers are out, both the umpires are gone
And there's been no play
Today,
There's been no play
As yet,
And it's wet. It's very wet.

So it's back to the chat again, will England bat again?
7 for 3,
That's bad.
The wicket's quite sticky (the cake's pretty icky).
Zimbabwe are plucky and jolly unlucky.
It's sad for Zimbabwe, it's sad.

But it has to be said (says Aggers to Fred)
That their timing's awry and they can't bat for toffee,
Old Cadders, old Goughy, they'll finish them off, eh?
Eh, Fred?
Eh, Fred?

Fred replies at some length on the relative strength
Of this England Eleven and one up in Heaven
That Fred can remember from 1907
When he was a lad.

Oh they knew how to play in those days, yes they did.
They'd be bowling all day for a couple of quid,
And a pint and a packet of fags.

They'd be up from the pits and they'd sluice off the nits,
Then they'd chuck all their togs in their bags
And off to the Test where they'd give of their best
Where they'd give it a go.

Is that so?
Says Aggers to Fred. Is that so?

Says Fred, yes they would, they were all bloody good,
They were right on the button, were Hammond and Hutton
And Hendren and Hobbs. And they'd play for the nobs
With lots of initials and not many jobs,
Yes they'd play, how they'd play
For A.P.F. Chapman and P.B.H. May,

For who did you say? says Aggers to Fred,

For P.G.H. Fender, R.W.V. Robins, R.E.S. Wyatt, J.W.H.T. Douglas, H.D.G.
Leveson-Gower, A.E.R. Gilligan, A.H.H. Gilligan, The Hon F.S.G. Calthorpe,
Old Uncle Plum Warner and all, old Uncle Plum Warner and all.

A marvellous crew, oh yes I'm telling you
They're a *marvellous* crew but they're dead.

Oh yes that's how it was in the old days,
The bold days, the gold days of yore
When England was England and gave them what-for.
If it came to the crunch and how.

But now?
It's a different ball game now

Fred shakes his head, takes the cake's last lusciousest slice.
Aaaaah that's nice. A ruminative munch.

It's a different ball-game now,
And how.
It's a different ball game now.

Zimbabwe are 7 for 3
And there's been no play since lunch.
But I think it's stopped raining,
Says Aggers.

                    Says Fred
Oh I'm not complaining,
Not I.
You never say die,
No you never say die,
No you *never* say die
Till you're dead.

So there's Cheggers and Duggers and Chuckers and Staggers,
There's Armpit and Buttock and Old Father Time.
There's a bottle of Bells on my knee.

Zimbabwe are 7 for 3.
And there's Mary MacPherson (there *is* such a person)
There's Mary MacPherson and me.

MATTHEW HARVEY
TRIBUTE TO BORGES

Borges climbed eleven blocks
He bent his head to sweeten grief
He turned a phrase and made his peace
With bamboo chairs and marble floors

The trees were green when Borges died
The world got up and went to work
The elder creatures did their sums
The bullies smirked

If all the time that Borges lived
Were to be compressed and sent abroad
And wrapped in brown and stamped: 'Take Care'
And left to roam

We'd find a finely carved timepiece
Ticking softly in a bar
Disguised behind a furrowed brow
And tenuous false beard

Now ninety years are waking up
And squinting in the Chinese sun
As Borges wrinkles restlessly
And fidgets in the grave

He turned a page and lost his sight
His enemies were dear to him
He lost his sight and found his way
Was dark as day and clear as night

For Borges tasted emptiness
He sent contraptions screaming home
He slept and dreamt for everyone
He severed hope

We do not know how Borges lived
The way he snapped and winked his eye
The way he licked his wicked lips
The way he cried

We know he died and did his best
He kept his head but lost his cool
We know he kept his silent vows
And played the fool

Now Borges whispers everywhere
The traffic drowns his trembling voice
And we who know but cannot tell
– O we of little choice –

The name of Borges on our lips
Our way of life in hand and rhyme
Jorge Luis Borges opens up
From time to time

The gap between, the space beneath
Jorge Luis Borges only knows
The way it tugs and laughs and bleeds
The way it goes

IN APPRECIATION OF

R. S. Thomas 1913–2000

by John Greening

QUITE OUT OF the blue, on the Sunday before his death, I had the most vivid dream about R. S. Thomas – so lucid that I told friends and colleagues about it on the Monday morning, and that evening took down his mighty *Collected Poems* to read again. I fell asleep re-reading them, and awoke next morning to the news.

The sort of experience that might fit snugly into the mythology of certain poets, perhaps, but I should imagine that most readers think of Thomas as pretty down-to-earth. Ted Hughes (one of his great fans) we eagerly associate with the apocrypha of buried amulets and fiery fox dreams. But R. S. Thomas? The disdain behind all those early parson-meets-peasant anthology pieces; the short shrift given to English visitors and water companies and biographers; those anecdotes about him deliberately parking his car in the middle of the road in Rhiw or sporting a sinister balaclava at a protest rally... Nothing of the New Age about him, no Celtic Twilight, no misty, quasi-spiritual ambience.

Yet, without resorting to the grand strains of Hopkins, or the teasing obscurities of Eliot, with no hint of Betjemanesque sentimentality, or the afflatus of Dylan, R. S. Thomas wrote of man's troubled relationship with God. And beyond the achievement of composing genuinely religious poetry adequate to (and relished by) a secular age, what is so remarkable about the poems he has left us – in particular, I think, those of his very last book, *No Truce with the Furies* – is that they speak directly without sacrificing any of the music. In fact, his work shows again and again how much essential poetry there is in the language even after the most ruthless paring away. That he possessed this gift for the inner music of English is, of course, the reason why he could never turn away from it, much as he laboured to woo the Welsh tongue, much as he hated the idea of one more powerful, more pushy language imposing itself on another. Perhaps he even saw an ironic parallel between his own task and that of the famous "prototype", Iago Prytherch: "chipping the green skin / From the yellow bones"

of the English language – though, not, naturally, with "a half-witted grin".

The facts of R. S. Thomas's life are well known and have been dealt with fully in the many warm obituaries (most memorably, I think, by Gwyneth Lewis in the *TLS*). The most thoroughgoing and entertaining exploration of the man's complexities came in Justin Wintle's 1996 "unauthorised biography": *Furious Interiors*, subtitled 'Wales, R. S. Thomas and God', from which one emerges with some picture of the difficulties facing future biographers. He glares from the cover (in Howard Barlow's photograph) through the open upper half of a stable door and we have no doubt that the unseen interiors are indeed furious. The dragon guards his hoard. It reminds me of that famous photograph of the aged Sibelius, reclusive and inspirationless at Järvenpää: the cameraman had simply captured a momentary disapproving frown, but it came to typify the Nordic legend and his Tuonelan mystery. R. S. Thomas was not a Welsh fire-breather (though he didn't object to the odd holiday cottage going up in smoke) and he composed some of the tenderest poems imaginable. I think of 'The Bright Field' or 'The Evacuee'. He was, however, a poet who looked at the world and at himself unflinchingly. And he did so right up until the end. There was no Sibelian thirty-year silence. One could even say he became a poetry machine, were that word *machine* not such an emotive one in his writings. But certainly there is something of Cynddylan on a Tractor about the poet sending the critics scattering with book after book into his mid-eighties. In the late 'Reflections' he looks in the mirror and sees:

There is no truce

with the furies. A mirror's temperature
is always at zero. It is ice
in the veins. Its camera
is an X-ray. It is a chalice

held out to you in
silent communion, where gaspingly
you partake of a shifting
identity never your own.

Looking again at that famous photograph of Howard Barlow's, it's worth remarking that R. S. Thomas is looking out, out past us and beyond. He is above all a poet who looked, who knew that one could "grow rich / With looking": at people, intermittently, but at landscape, at trees, most passionately at birds... Although he wrote less about these things than about paintings, churches, music, myth, history, ideas, ideas of nationhood and theology, the idea of looking itself. The topics and the paradoxes are too numerous to mention, but of course paradox is the stuff of poetry, too. And the poetry is what we are left with, thank God.

I remember an essay by John Wain in which he quoted Thomas's poem 'Via Negativa' as an example "of the damage caused to a poet's work by the flight from form". Yet this poem, like so many of his, seems to me to gather to a form as iron filings do on a page above a magnet. There is never any doubt that the shaping spirit of imagination is at work. 'Via Negativa' uses, in fact, a characteristically lively enjambment: the end of each line a cliff we might possibly throw ourselves off, a question which only God – or the succeeding line can answer. And it is this ability to keep us on the edge – within sight of common sense, within earshot of resolution, on the edge of finally *knowing* – together with his superb syntactical control and purity of diction, that gives his poems the power to "endure", like Iago Prytherch, long after our more curious stars have guttered out.

Yehuda Amichai 1924 – 2000

by Elaine Feinstein

IRONIC, MOVING, EMINENTLY sane, Yehuda Amichai's poems are among the most memorable of the last century. Comparable only to poets of Eastern and Central Europe like Zbigniew Herbert, Miroslav Holub and Vasco Popa, all now sadly dead, Amichai was, like them, at once the voice of his embattled people and a vital presence in world poetry. He belonged to the generation of Jews who ran away from the Nazi terror in Germany to Israel in the Thirties, and had to try and build a new life in an ancient land. In the process, he and his fellow writers transformed Biblical Hebrew into a witty, slangy language that could deal with difficult times. Amichai was pre-eminent as a poet, and the best of Israel as a man. He knew about wars, and how little pity God shows to the men who fight in them; he had fought in five himself. He knew both about rifles hidden away in closets of lingerie, and men crawling in their own blood over desert sand. He writes about the pain of soldiers, and the even

greater desolation of those whose sons are lost on the battlefield; his imagery is so casual it seems almost invisible. When he meets Mr Beringer, who lost his son in the battle of the Suez canal, for instance, Amichai observes:

He has grown very thin, has lost
the weight of his son.

He lived in Jerusalem and knew how hard it was to breathe an air so saturated in prayers and dreams. For a human being to try and run Jerusalem seemed to him a sad absurdity:

How can any man be the Mayor of a city like that ?
What can he do with her?
He will build, and build, and build

And at night
The stones of the hills round about

Will crawl down
Towards the stone houses
Like wolves coming
To howl at the dogs
who have become men's slaves.

His understanding stretches back through the long history of the Jewish people to draw on legends embodied in the biblical language of Hebrew itself. And like any Jew, secular or not, his poems argue with God; about his purposes, his ruthlessness, the demands he puts on the whole human race.

Amichai's awareness of cruelty leads him to prize gentleness above all virtues : he writes lovingly of his father, for instance, because he remembers being woken early, as a child, with a stroke on his fore-head, rather than a blanket pulled from his sleeping body. His own tenderness brings a peculiar inten-sity to family love. In a lyric in which the eyes of each of his children are compared to the fruits of the season in which they were born, he concludes

And all are sweet in my worry.
And the eyes of the Lord roam the earth.
And my eyes are always looking round my house.
God's in the eye business and the fruit business
I'm in the worry business.

The black humour of the diaspora is transfigured in Amichai's quiet voice, yet his unhappiness is always tinged with humour. The town he was born in has been destroyed by shells, the ship on which he sailed to Israel was sunk in the Second World War, a barn where he made love, and a foot bridge in Ismailia have both been blown up. Yet he writes without self-pity:

The girl from my childhood was killed and my father
                                                           is dead.
That's why you should never choose me
To be a lover or a son or a bridge crosser
Or a citizen or a tenant

Human love in all its aspects, sometimes erotic, sometimes poignant, is Amichai's finest subject. Reflecting on the end of his first marriage, for instance, he writes of his hips having been ampu-tated from his wife's thighs by surgical violence:

A pity. We were such a good
And loving invention,
An airplane made from a man and a wife
Wings and everything.
We hovered a little above the earth.
We even flew a little

About tourists who love to visit the Middle East – unless of course the situation on the ground looks risky – Amichai had his reservations. He finds them likely to be more interested in archaeology than living human beings:

They squat on the Holocaust Memorial
They put on grave faces at the Wailing Wall

It would be redemption of a kind, he suggests, if tour guides could begin to say : "You see that arch from the Roman period? That's not important. But next to it, left and down a bit, there sits a man who's bought fruit and vegetables for his family".

Amichai was a humanist without much time for ideology; his experience had taught him that in poli-tics there are few happy endings. Popa's Yugoslavia and Amichai's Israel both fell into civil violence almost immediately after the death of their coun-tries' leading poets. Only Holub lived to see Czechoslovakia prosper, and to die at the height of his own personal optimism. Amichai wrote out of a tradition that put a high value on peace. Yet surely what would have distressed him most, if he had lived, would have been the lack of understanding with which the present conflict is being interpreted.

His poems translate brilliantly – as Herbert's and Holub's do – because he had absolutely no interest in poetic decoration and always went straight for the central image. In that, the poetry is like the man. No doubt the translation is easier, too, because modern Hebrew poems use open forms, and Amichai himself was soaked in the tradi-tion of contemporary poetry written in English. It is rare to recommend books of translations as if they were original poems, but here I can do so with confidence. His *Selected Poems* (Faber and Faber, £9.99), have been chosen by Ted Hughes, who translated many of them himself, and Daniel Weissbort. The book came out a few weeks after his death, and remains a delight.

THE REVIEW PAGES

Desperately Seeking Sylvia

JANE HARDY ON THE MULTI-FACETED ICON

The Journals of Sylvia Plath

Ed. Karen V. Kukil
Faber, £30
ISBN 0 571 19704 3

ERICA WAGNER

Ariel's Gift

Faber, £14.99
ISBN 0 571 20085 0

P. RAJANI

The Poetry of Sylvia Plath

Sangam, £11.95
ISBN 0 86311 848 8

ONE OF THE problems with trying to get to the heart of Sylvia Plath is that there are so many of her, so many Sylvias. Her personality included ecstatic Sivvy writing letters home to her mother about achievements and suppressing the dark moods; the model and journalist trying out May Ball gowns for *Varsity*; the serious student and writer; the married woman (half of "the writing Hughes" as she proudly describes herself and new husband Ted Hughes); the mother; and, of course, the suicide. Not to mention the diarist, always trying to make sense of herself and the world.

The Journals of Sylvia Plath, covering the years 1950-1962 and finally published earlier this year, are perhaps the best place to look for this multi-faceted, now iconic poet. Like Whitman, Plath contains multitudes. Unlike Whitman's, hers are internal, possibly to counter the emptiness she felt throughout her adult life. As early as November 1950, in among a glorious jumble of adolescent thoughts about boys and the meaning of life, Sylvia Plath writes, " – God, who am I? I sit in the library tonight, the lights glaring overhead, the fan whirring loudly. Girls, girls everywhere reading books. Intent faces, flesh pink, white, yellow. And I sit here without identity: faceless". Planning her future, in August 1950, Plath exclaims, "Why can't

I try on different lives, like dresses, to see which fits best and is most becoming?" She tried on and wore numerous identities over the intense years, rather like Elastoplasts on a deep cut.

But the voice – or voices – remains strong. The sense of self dominates from early on. Plath knew her vocation, to write, and put it down to a "habit of introversion, brought up as I was in the world of Mary Poppins and Winnie-the-Pooh..." She starts one diary entry at Smith with an account of snow, hears someone shouting "Oh, look at it!" and notes "But I have been looking for some time now". She never stopped looking and part of the appeal of this account of a growing up, a maturing mind – Holden Caulfield without the humour? – is seeing what she saw. There is a slight smugness, too, but of course Sylvia Plath knew herself so well, she spotted this. After describing her sense of difference from the other students, all with competing egos, she writes: "But I am I now... I: how firm a letter; how reassuring the three strokes: one vertical, proud and assertive, and then the two short horizontal lines in quick, smug succession. The pen scratches on the paper...I...I...I...I...I...I". But in the next entry, Plath shows her other side, the judgmental self which never let her feel entirely satisfied with things for long. "I think I am worthwhile just because I have optical nerves and can try to put down what they perceive. What a fool!"

This wearying dance between satisfaction and self-criticism, joy and fear, is a thread through the *Journals*. After her first important acceptance, when Harper's magazine bought three poems for $100, Sylvia exults in "the unforgettable snatching of toothpicks and olive pits from the tables of the ambrosial gods!" And in that ironic image shows how fragile she felt her success to be.

Acting almost as light relief after the conflict between these two voices, the sensitive observer and harsh critic, is the girlish voice. When Plath describes men, dresses, the female side of life in a gushing manner, you remember she spent a summer working at the woman's magazine

Mademoiselle. On 13 May, 1953, not long before her first attempt to kill herself, she describes an early bout of retail therapy: "Yesterday I bought a raincoat with a frivolous pink lining that does good to my eyes because I have never had anything pink-colored, and it was much too expensive". She adds that it cost a month's pay, "and soon I will not have any money to do anything more with because I am buying clothes because I love them and they are exactly right, if I pay enough". The physical appearance of things counts with Plath, even at key moments in her life, such as the account of her first kiss from Ted Hughes. Here her red scarf seems woven into the moment, "my lovely red hairband scarf which has weathered the sun and much love". This fashion journalist's description alongside the emotional history strangely makes the passionate and brutal kiss, with the bite, the blood and Hughes ripping off the scarf, more poignant.

Plath's varying prose styles often carry heavy psychological freight. And although the *Journals* are much more than a case history, the states of this over-sensitive mind are revealed in the raw via the writing. At times, there is a painful imaginative overload – you can sense it in the overlong, quarter-page sentences. Sometimes she seems unable to take a breath in her keenness to pin everything down. This is writing without proportion, with Plath unable and unwilling to leave things out. There are examples everywhere, but typical is her journal fragment detailing a Paris trip at the end of 1955. "New Year's Eve: 1956... Carrying bags, square gray vanity case, olivetti, black umbrella, climbing steep steps to train, lugging cases, compartments filling with joking sailors in blue, stocky wrinkled peasants pulling ham sandwiches out of bulky leather bags", and so on for a couple of pages. Comparing Plath's journals with Virginia Woolf's equally famous diaries, there is in the more elegant prose the same fluster of subordinate clauses when Woolf felt under mental pressure, the same desire to see and convey it all. And sometimes there is almost too much detail in this lightly edited sprawl of a book. The reader can become obsessive too, equally absorbed by Sylvia'a account of the joys of nose-picking as by her emotional neediness.

The dark voice is, of course, always strong. While still describing the train journey to Paris, Plath replicates the rhythm of the "wheels, clacking out nursery rhymes, summing up the moments of the mind like the chant of a broken record: saying over and over: god is dead, god is dead, going,

going, going". Sylvia Plath was what psychiatrists now call a "borderline" personality, somebody neither neurotic nor psychotic but on the edge. Marilyn Monroe was another example. Depression is obviously a recurring leitmotif, but even here what is unexpected is the force of the writing. Plath is Lady Lazarus, doing depression "so well it feels like hell... so well it feels real". As critic Al Alvarez (who knew Plath and Hughes and published several poems from *Ariel* in *The Observer* days after Sylvia's death) notes in his autobiography, "(But) the poems she wrote in her suicidal depression are sardonic, angry, unforgiving, tender, yet disciplined and always curiously detached; they are full of life, not death". The same is true of the *Journals*. It's significant that Plath frequently uses birth imagery to describe her pain, for example when coming to terms with her rejection by her college boyfriend Richard Norton. Even when talking about her depressive paralysis and stasis, Plath produces the words to bring these states to life.

Sylvia Plath's *Journals* are also a revealing companion – almost a gloss – to her poetry. You can trace in them the development of her distinctive diction and symbolism. A little later on her train journey to France, she sees the Mediterranean. "The Cote d'Azur. A new country, a new year: spiked with green explosions of palms, cacti sprouting vegetable octopuses with spiky tentacles, and the red sun rising like the eye of God out of a screaming blue sea". The tone is straight out of *Ariel*. She rehearses other poetic characteristics, such as her individual views of colours, in her diaries. The sinister aspect of white, for example, a no-colour which haunts poems such as 'The Munich Mannequins' and 'Tulips', is early identified with destruction. After describing the first snow at Smith, Plath moves into her interpretation. The house opposite her digs is "melting and crumbling into whiteness", a kind of last state, and then she sees a more apocalyptic end. "Now there is a stippling of white caught on the edge of things, and I wonder what would happen to us all if the planes came, and the bombs".

Similarly, there are try-outs for recurring symbols such as the malevolent eye, hospital images. Plath's poetry is not compressed in the Emily Dickinson way, but through the creation of a powerful personal symbolic language. As Alvarez points out, the poets of what he calls the Age of Anxiety, Lowell, Berryman and Plath, wrote not in confessional style but a hard, "classical" manner.

Unsurprisingly, Ted Hughes was strongly affected by reading the journals. In *Birthday Letters*, he presents his long-awaited side of the story with skill and some special pleading. In 'Visit', he remembers throwing stones up at Plath's window one night she was out – and adds:

Ten years after your death
I meet on a page of your journal, as never before,
The shock of your joy
When you heard of that.

He registers the intensity with which Sylvia wanted this relationship with him. She'd prayed that he would feature in her life, "And under those prayers your panic". To elucidate more of the Hughes-Plath conjunction, there's now *Ariel's Gift*. Whether we need this extra book, neatly but speedily written by *The Times*' Literary Editor Erica Wagner, is a moot point. There are valuable insights and readings of Hughes' poems but it is also part of the Plath industry whose chief activity sometimes seems to be reading her work through her life. There is even a grotesque sense that Plath's suffering was in ratio to the excellence of her writing. And worse, a sense that the excellence of her final work almost justifies or compensates for the sad ending to her life.

But this image of the tormented, post-Romantic artist doesn't quite fit. Plath was happy to plunder her own life and experience for her art. Erica Wagner quotes Judith Kroll, who rightly says, "It is important to separate the aesthetic sense of her (Plath's) poems from the biography, on which it does not depend". Of course, *Birthday Letters* as a book does depend on Plath's and Hughes' life, which is ultimately a weakness. His poems point us back to this self-dramatising, ultimately very alive figure. There is a kind of odd resurrection sense here – Plath's contemporary voice is reinvented 40 years on and still reaches us alive, singing and suffering. In fact, she has attained a kind of new iconic status with successive generations. On the back of the novel *Prozac Nation* a reviewer was quoted as saying "Sylvia Plath with the ego of Madonna", confident today's readers would get the point.

Plath definitely stands for vulnerability in the twentieth-century pantheon. Yet she was primarily a writer with a ruthless sense that everything could be good copy. Even, or especially the downside of life. On the decline and eventual death of a neighbour in Devon, she showed a reporter's curiosity as well as sympathy. This old man, Percy Key, collapsed one day in a supposed stroke. Plath's reaction when his wife Rose called for help from Ted Hughes was revealing. First she thinks she'll let her husband deal with it, then "I thought I would stay and wait, and then something in me said, now, you must see this, you have never seen a stroke or a dead person. So I went..." Her description of the man's state is clear-eyed, objective to the point of inhumanity. "Percy was in his chair in front of the television set, twitching in a fearsome way, utterly gone off, mumbling over what I thought must be his false teeth, his eyes twitching askew, and shaking as if pierced by weak electric shocks". It's a good, detailed eye-witness account, with the false teeth picked out as a kind of metonymy. She returns to the teeth when recording her and Hughes' reaction away from the scene. "I have been waiting for this, I said. And Ted said he had, too". Then she is horrified, seized by "dry retching" at the thought of "that horrible mumbling over false teeth. A disgust".

The poem 'Berck-plage' (from *Ariel*) makes confident use of this experience. And since this is art, not reportage, the material shifts and slots into Plath's characteristic nightmare-landscape where the "many-snaked" sea retreats hissing, leaving behind thoughts of death and decay. The dead man's appearance goes in almost unaltered from the *Journal* entries. But the meaning has moved on – "this is what it is to be complete. It is horrible" – she adds after the real detail of a book being used to prop up the dead man's stiffening jaw.

Plath squeezed life. The perfectionism she aimed at was an ideal, but also "horrible" like Percy's unnatural death-hardened jaw. The *Journals* is a big book with big themes, among them the debate on the relationship between art and life. Plath captured both, and there is a marvellous strand of sensuality here. She notes good lovemaking as well as good writing.

In a sense, we do not do justice to Sylvia Plath's writing via dry dissection (see P. Rajani's recently published *The Poetry of Sylvia Plath* with its emphasis on pinning each line to a biographical detail or emotion or critical opinion) or over-biographical emphasis. And we shouldn't always start at the end, her death. Her daughter Frieda made this point recently in an article in *The Times* magazine on the reason she fought to have her mother's blue plaque erected on a flat where she'd lived with Hughes and not on the flat in NW3 where she spent her last few months. It is difficult to read Plath innocently, but maybe we should try. We owe her that.

His Lyric Care

by Ian Tromp

DOUGLAS DUNN

The Year's Afternoon
Faber, £7.99
ISBN 0 57 1 20427 9

THREE WORDS RECUR in several of Douglas Dunn's new poems: fortitude, kindness, and lyrical (or lyric). These words accurately characterise the book's tone, encompassing its gentler and its harder passages – for the book has these two aspects: delicacy and stoniness, or (to borrow Dunn's own description of Norman MacCaig's verse) "Lyric intelligence... ringed with fire".

In 'A European Dream', Dunn refers to "my sturdy aphorism": to " 'Feel hard and think historical' ". This poem represents the second aspect, the harder side of his verse, with its grimness and grit. Its oneiric wandering through recent European history is uncompromised, uncompromising; and its imagery in the end is dark:

It is disagreeable, to tend your garden, on your
                                                                    knees,
With the sensation of tending millions of graves.

But it would be too easy, since this poem exerts such a weight on the reader's consciousness, to focus on this side of Dunn's work over the more intimate, more delicate aspect. Even in this poem, he speaks of a "Hunger for lyrical anger"; in a sense this quote describes even the hardest of his poems, for their anger is based in lyricism, their hardness in graceful form and expression. And the poem serves, too, to demonstrate another aspect of *The Year's Afternoon*: Dunn's poems occasionally spark with a knowing, understated humour, as in his description of the dreamer:

in my thornproof Border tweeds,
My briefcase and umbrella, as my Scottish brogues
leathered the tarmac, a credit to Hoggs of Fife.

There are three poems in particular which seem expressions of Dunn's poetic credo, 'Teachers', 'Martagon Lilies', and 'Leopardi'. For the last of

these alone, *The Year's Afternoon* would be worth reading, but it is in the first of the three that he most clearly describes his intentions and his sense of values in poetry:

Love above all, its who, its when and where
Melting in local light and circumstance,
Can find their meaning in *my* lyric care –
Not politics only, but time and chance,

Reality's garden, no scunner in it,
The indefinite and the infinite
In a large phrase. And all that's what I want,
Beginning in a language I can trust
As mine, live in it, hide there, sing, or flaunt,
Not what I'm told to say, but what I must.

This closing insistence on writing in "a language I can trust / As mine" links to the presence of Scotland in many poems, and the presence of Scots in a few (embodied here in the internal half-rhyme of "... where / ... care / ... scunner ..."). The River Tay appears in a number of poems, linking language to landscape (most evocatively, in 'Night Watch' Dunn wonders "How many tons of Tay / pass silently"), and in 'The Black Douglas', he apostrophises his homeland, "yelling 'Scotland! / I'm doing my best and my worst! Hallelujah!'".

This last poem follows immediately on 'Three Poets', Dunn's elegy for MacCaig, Sorley MacLean and George Mackay Brown, the three Scottish poets who died in 1996, "a very bad year for the deaths of poets". The poem recalls the three lost writers, beginning with a chorus and ending with an epilogue enjoining readers to "sit quietly and read" and finally to toast their memory: "Come, friends, let us drink to our nation's finest men. / Let us drink to them. Then let us drink to them again". Each of the middle sections rejoices in and recalls one of the three poets. The intimacy of these brief portraits is affecting, and leaves the reader with a sense of the sadness of the loss of these men – though Dunn's main focus is on the loss to poetry, and specifically to the poetry of Scotland, the strength of feeling called forth clearly rings with the sorrow of lost friendship. One could so easily mistake Dunn's tone here, and elsewhere in the book, for melancholy. But in the love expressed in 'Three Poets', and the appreciation of beauty in 'Martagon Lilies' and 'Early Hours in Dairsie', for instance, one realises that the emotion that characterises so much of his verse is, rather, nostalgia – or to use a Gaelic word Dunn would surely recognise, "*cianalas*". The etymology of these words is similar: both stand for the painful condition of being away from one's home, of being separated from the scenes, the streets, the hillsides and streams, the people one longs for.

The closing lines of the wonderful 'Leopardi' again express Dunn's vision for poetry, when he calls upon:

> a sense of art
> Which says its purpose is to raise soul up
> While also pleasing us, and breaking the heart.

This, for me, perfectly evokes the tenor of the best of the poems here. And in a sense, too, it returns us to the three words that recur in this book – fortitude, kindness, and lyrical. For what raises the soul gives it courage and fortitude, and few things please us humans as kindness does – and the lyric grace of the best of Dunn's verse is heartbreakingly tender.

Rough Guide to Wales

by Douglas Houston

Oxygen

Ed. Amy Wack and Grahame Davies

Seren, £9.95.

ISBN 18541 2848

THIS COLLECTION OF work by thirty-one younger poets from Wales contains a stimulating variety of material, much of it fresh with the energies of new poetic talents excited at discovering their potential. It's also refreshing to find an anthology that overrides the linguistic split in Wales's cultural identity by offering poetry in both Welsh and English. Verse by the fifteen poets working in Welsh appears with parallel English translations, giving English language readers a ready point of access to the subjects and, as far as translation may contrive, the styles and tones of contemporary Welsh poetry. The translations, many by the original authors, are impressive, the results in English often forming admirably versified poems in themselves.

Differences of idiom are discernible through the veil of translation between the Welsh and English poetries. The work originating in the Welsh language carries a greater confidence of address within a constituency defined by the demographically precarious status of the language within Wales. Irony seems less endemic than in contemporary English verse, a consequence of diminished anxiety over the nature of poetic identity enjoyed by poets writing out of the traditional continuities of Welsh culture. An acknowledgement of the marginal character of that culture is repeatedly conveyed by the Welsh poems. As Grahame Davies puts it in 'Rough Guide',

> I'm the Wandering Welshman.
> I'm Jewish everywhere.
> Except, of course, in Israel.
> There I'm Palestinian.

(author's translation)

Gwyneth Lewis has the distinction of being the only contributor working in both Welsh and English and she is well represented by poems in both languages. With Oliver Reynolds, Paul Henry, and Stephen Knight, each of whom has poems in *Oxygen*, Lewis has already established a reputation that carries far beyond the cultural and geographical borders of Wales. Good selections, including previously uncollected poems, have been made from the works of these poets, who contribute their share to the buoyancy of the anthology as a whole. It's exhilarating to re-read such flagrantly successful pieces as Lewis's 'Pentecost' and Knight's 'After Lessons'.

The range of the work collected extends from such achieved examples of what poetry is capable of today through to the less stable products of poets still engaged in exploratory flexings of their talents. There's a tendency for some poems to seem too eager to happen, manner outrunning matter as the energies of enthusiastic composition push an intuition or idea a little further than it ought to go. Don Rodgers's 'The Suffering of Fishes', for example, would have made a lively three or four stanzas, but loses impact with five. He shows what he's really capable of in 'The Big Battalions', a poem of considerable solidity and poise which rises splendidly to the occasion of its imaginatively estranging rendering of our lives and times. Similarly, Anna Wigley's 'Duck Shooting' stands out as a compelling and entirely successful poem among her other less focused contributions.

These two and others who have yet to be more widely heard of maintain an encouragingly high level of technique. If some of their poems fail to convince, they retain the virtues and interest of being well made. A clear sense of the line as the primary unit of verse prevails and well-shaped stanzas, often with good use of rhyme, are the order of the day in *Oxygen*. Strengths of precision and economy are evident throughout and the book contains work from poets whose worth is likely to be proved in due course.

Owen Sheers, Sarah Corbett, and Kate Bingham, three of the youngest poets in the collection, has each published a well received first collection. Sheers is at his best with 'Night Bus', which interweaves an intense evocation of the mundane urban limbo suggested by its title with an intermittent narrative of a random erotic encounter. In this poem, subject and setting are subordinated to the imagination's work of figuring an epiphany of love through the details, moods, and atmospheres presented. Sheers's other poems are powerful and well judged, but can seem constrained by the conscientiousness with which he addresses particular topics.

There's an occasionally unsettling imaginative vitality to Sarah Corbett's poems here, a frisson of taboos being broken in the intensely sensual imagery of poems like 'My Mother's Lover'. Her innate grasp of strong form gives structure to the wilder energies of her verse. The closing stanza of 'My Son the Horse', for example, achieves its resonance and dramatic finality through the keenness of Corbett's ear in managing the stresses of the closing lines:

In three years I will break him.
We will ride the high hill.
What power we will own
When his broad back strengthens.

'Oxygen' by Kate Bingham, which gives the anthology its title, is that rare thing, a readable, entertaining, and otherwise worthwhile poem about the business of poetic composition. The poem's sustained metaphor of space flight gives it

similarity to her 'In Passing' and 'How to Play', both of which deftly extend the rather abstract conceptions out of which they grow. These poems have a wit and agility of language that is absent from Bingham's more autobiographical pieces, which can lapse into a comparatively prosaic loyalty to fact.

Samantha Wynne Rhydderch and Fiona Sampson are the most notable of the less widely published poets present. Both produce work marked by the verve and precision with which syntax, image, and rhythm interact in lines of spiky originality:

My bones
In triplicate have nowhere to hide.
Their fragility becomes heraldic

When these exegetes invoke them
in Latin

That's from Rhydderch's 'The X-Ray Room', which shares its effectively phantasmagoric aspects with her 'The Lighthouse Keeper's Daughter' and 'The Breakdown', two powerful treatments of mental disturbance. 'The Phone Book Errata' is altogether lighter, and serves a socially therapeutic function in getting its laugh at the expense of BT and its plague of recorded announcements.

Fiona Sampson has a superb poem in 'Pastoral from a Millennial Pattern Book', perfectly balancing its remoter imaginative and intellectual perspectives with a richness of earthy, ordinary detail. The last two lines do the work of closure wonderfully, rounding the poem out with a persuasive touch of aphoristic inevitability: "...and every pastoral returns to loss,/cow-like, with conscientious care". She's at her best when her scrupulous diction gives the substance of felt experience to the analytical drive characteristically underlying her verse, as in the negative adumbration of solitude in 'About the House':

But nothing comes in.
No comprehensive palliative word
Comes in like an embrace; the skin of no meaning
Touches my arm below the sleeve.

Karen Goodwin and Zoe Skoulding must also be mentioned among the lesser-known poets included in the anthology. The former's 'Wolf and 'The Sin Eaters' are vividly imaginative treatments written with convincing pace and force. Skoulding's 'Eclipse' is one of the best poems in the book, audaciously conflating images of the First World War with responses to the 1999 eclipse of

the sun. Work like theirs exemplifies the combination of promise and achievement that is stimulatingly evident throughout the poetry of the younger contributors to *Oxygen*.

Barnardine's Reply

by John Goodby

The Thing About Roy Fisher

Ed. John Kerrigan and Peter Robinson

Critical Studies series, Liverpool University Press, £34.99
ISBN 085323525 2

News for the ear: A homage to Roy Fisher

Ed. Robert Sheppard and Peter Robinson

Stride Publications, £8.95
ISBN 1 900152 67 3

ROY FISHER IS seventy this year, and the two volumes under review here celebrate that fact and offer, for the first time, book-length introductions to his formidable *oeuvre*. In the thirteen pieces assembled by John Kerrigan and Peter Robinson (which include an exhaustive bibliography compiled by Derek Slade), scrupulous attention is paid to virtually every phase of Fisher's nearly fifty years of poetic output, allowing us to trace a narrative of poetic development which has been exemplary in its rigour and consistency. The *festschrift*, which is almost entirely free of the kind of gush usually found in such things, offers prose and verse tributes by fellow poets, and a wittily thought-provoking memoir by, and interview with, Fisher himself. The general effect of both books is of a consensus among critics and writers of very divergent opinions and practices which says much for the stature of a poet once paradoxically described as "famous for having been largely ignored".

Such "ignorance", and its gradual overcoming, inevitably begs questions concerning the ways in which English poetry has understood itself since World War II. Originating in the post-Apocalypse, pre-Movement window of opportunity which saw several poets adopting internationalist and experimental perspectives – think of Edwin Morgan,

Christopher Middleton and Ian Hamilton Findlay – Fisher's modernism made him an outsider to the Movement and post-Movement mainstream, finding his audience in the counter-cultural and small press movement in the UK and Beat and Black Mountain-influenced US equivalent. Yet his work was neither Creeley-minimalist nor Ginsberg-expansivist, marked as it was by a restless variety of forms and genres: *City* (1961) is a collage of prose, free verse and lyric in surrealist, expressionist and documentary modes, *The Ship's Orchestra* (1966) and *The Cut Pages* (1971) are experimental prose works, and the pieces in *The Memorial Fountain* (1967) combine realist exactitude with disorienting linguistic scepticism. Though linked with Cid Corman, Gael Turnbull and Denise Levertov, Fisher was nevertheless beholden to no-one for a style which was both cerebral and yet often "appetitive and involvingly injured". In the late 1970s he quietly consolidated his achievement with two *Collected*s, having already brought one out in 1968, switched to OUP, and in 1986 published *A Furnace*, the intricately-structured, seven-part quasi-epic considered by many to be his masterpiece. Some work in *Birmingham River* (1994) can be read as an abandonment of modernism, although it says more about versatility than retreat, and about the ongoing fascination with the city of his birth.

Just as his poetry often seems to problematise its rendering of realist surfaces and discursive syntax with modernist epistemological scepticism and play, so Fisher's unstable reputation has challenged the narrowness of the poetic mainstream. Both Donald Davie's attempt in 1974 to align it to a Hardyesque tradition, and the interest generated by a newer, more plural and postmodernised mainstream in the 1980s, bore witness to a need to acknowledge Fisher's presence, even as the haphazard nature of the acknowledgement served to underline the degree of lip-service involved. Recent advocates – most notably Ian Gregson – have read Fisher in the light of Russian Formalism's focus on "estrangement", his modernism enabled by being able to "brace itself against" his materialist realism (for Gregson, "Fisher knows brick the way an Eskimo knows snow"), each aspect unsettling the other to produce poetry which follows the processes of perception. This is illuminating, but finally a little too pat and neatly balanced to explain the darker, phobic elements of the early poetry in particular. One virtue of the Kerrigan-Robinson book is that it problematises the place-and-perception staples of Fisher criticism. In his chapter on the importance of place in Fisher's writing, Kerrigan himself properly relates the metamorphic strategies of the poetry to Birmingham's regular raze-and-rebuild cycle; but he also links the "technically extreme" poetry to his setting of location in perceptual and psychological spheres, his exploration of how the senses construct space and attempts to "think beyond three dimensions". Our appreciation of the neurasthenic quality this hints at is extended by James Keery, who also gives it some historical context when he claims a continuity between Apocalypse and figures such as Ted Hughes, revealing in the process that Dylan Thomas, of all people, was an inspiration for the young Fisher. Lighter, but scarcely lightweight, are chapters by John Lucas and Ian Sansom which discuss the importance of jazz and humour in Fisher and nicely leaven the generally dense texture. Traces of either might have helped the piece by Ian F. A. Bell and Meriel Lland, which rather relentlessly nails Fisher's "osmotic investigations" to William James's *The Principles of Psychology*; but this is an exception which proves the generally very readable rule of the book.

Simon Jarvis, Robert Sheppard and Marjorie Perloff explore the more experimental poetry and its relationship to Fisher's struggle with writer's block in the late 1960s. As an adolescent who had already enjoyed *City*, encountering such mid-period work in Kingstanding Public Library (about three miles from Fisher's Handsworth as the 91 bus crawls), I remember being thrown almost completely by the 'Interiors' sequence:

> Experimenting, experimenting,
>   with long damp fingers twisting
>   all the time and in the dusk
> White like unlit electric bulbs she said
> "This green goes with this purple", the hands going,
> The question pleased: "Agree?"

A woman cuts the speaker's hair in a bedsit; the mood is one of menace stirred with deadpan black humour. Fine; but then the poem undermines its visualisable location as well as its lyric voice; walls vanish, the ground opens up, banal objects – light-bulbs, chairs – circulate. With the benefit, later, of an English degree, it would be possible to detect *Portrait of a Lady*'s lilac-twisting, Rimbaud's 'Chercheuses des poux' and the Surrealist's use of hair as a metonym of female sexual desire, even maybe spot that its prosody was inspired by Wittgenstein's numbered propositions in the *Tractacus*. But in itself this would not have helped much. On the other hand, a rationale for Fisher's growing distrust of language can be found in 'It is Writing', with its need to

> …mistrust the poem in its hour of success,
> a thing capable of being
> tempted by ethics into the wonderful.

In a witty gloss on an early image – "The secret laugh of the world picks them up and shakes them like peas boiling" – Sansom wittily calls its "comic turn on Eliot's high-flown theologizing (in *Burnt Norton*)" a "swapping [of] a bird's eye view for a Bird's Eye view". But this kind of irony would not be an option from the mid-1960s onwards, as Fisher attempted to slough off his earlier "unwilling hero" stance and come to terms with a more provisional subjectivity. Simon Jarvis discusses the resultant "blockage", not only as subjective difficulty but as "the blocked experience of every living subject under the cult of indifference" in late capitalist society. That is, he links Fisher's habitual to-and-fro movement "from object to subject", between "realism" and "formalism", to a dispiriting postwar society and its embodiment in the built environment. As he points out, buying into the dominant discursive-realist styles of that society carries the danger of surrender to officialdom's "indifferent nihilism"; yet an oppositional poetics of disconnection threatens to deliver the poem to the different unfreedom of existence as a collection of "inert bits". This is the dilemma enacted by the voice in 'The Only Image':

> The salts I can compare
> To anything there is.
> Anything.

Here it is impossible to tell "whether this is an emancipation or an imprisonment"; the "abstract freedom" to compare anything with anything else mimics a world in which all values are exchange, rather than use values.

Such problems erupted in 1970 in *The Cut Pages*, Fisher's most formally audacious work. Although it broke his block, he has never republished it. The essays suggest why; a limit text, it marks a point beyond which Fisher was not prepared to go. Marjorie Perloff's essay gives an American perspective on this, suggesting that the work anticipates L=A=N=G=U=A=G=E poetics, following which Fisher became more "conventional". Sheppard agrees, citing Rosmarie Waldrop and Jackson Mac Low as Fisher's (unwitting) poetic progeny; he is also the only contributor to discuss at length the one other work by Fisher which approaches *The Cut Pages*' formalism, *The Ship's Orchestra*. For Sheppard, Fisher's prose works are hybrids, lacking the formalisation of prose fiction or the fluidity of prose poetry proper, crucial in the investigation of his phobias, of improvisational possibilities and the integrity of the observing self. The worry in this, however – greater in Perloff than in Sheppard – is the implication of an evolutionary, onward and upward narrative, which Fisher's very mixed practices resist.

Given Fisher's anti-authoritarianism, it might seem strange that what he sees as his major achievement makes mysticism central to its operations. *A Furnace*, which "superimposes" the landscapes of Birmingham on those of the rural north-west corner of Staffordshire where Fisher now lives, and takes the form of a section cut through a double spiral, receives – rightly, I feel – more attention than any other single work. The "furnace" of its title refers to the poem's processing of "obstinate substances" through decay and reshaping, of cities, people or anything else for that matter, and points to Fisher's persistent concern with last things (the subject, appropriately enough, of the last chapter, by Peter Robinson). Ralph Pite's discussion of the influence of John Cowper Powys, the poem's dedicatee, draws attention to Powys's animism and links it to Fisher's refusal of instrumental language, his countenancing of what is called elsewhere the poem's "attempt to think beyond religious schema about mysteries which have been enlarged rather than resolved by the advance of scientific knowledge". *A Furnace*'s chief concern is with the dissolution of boundaries and compartmentalising modes of thought, and in particular that which separates the living and the dead. Clair Wills remarks a "gothic aura" proportionate to Fisher's

insistence that rationalism can never finally eliminate the supernatural. The urge to call up the lost, mute generations leads him to populate the spaces of the poem with presences, but in a quasi-pagan manner which avoids both Christian consolation and stoical atheistic denial. If this is unusual in English writing, there are, as Wills notes, some striking parallels in Irish writing. In Fisher's case, however, the message of the dead is unapocalyptic, their haunting rooted in humdrum amnesia rather than trauma. Nevertheless, the very inconspicuousness of these ghosts is what should shock; for if the dead continually influence the living, Fisher implies, then so many of the living live a death in life. Yet to memorialise these ghosts would be to inflict another death, and the poem's solution lies in noting the ceaseless interchange between living and dead, suggesting gently that that which is lost is not necessarily vanished. This process is embodied, for Fisher, in its modern guise, in the rise and decline of the great industrial cities, of which Birmingham is exemplary. At the close of the poem, however, as if to suggest that this is still too close for us to grasp the connection, he offers an image of an ancient Roman settlement in Catalonia as it succumbs to snail-like colonisation:

> The snails ascend
>
>   the thin clear light,
> taking their spirals higher;
>   in the dusk
> luminous white, clustered
> like seed-pods of some other plant;
> quietly
> rasping their way round
>   together, and upward;
> tight and seraphic.

Reading such a passage, so verbally alert and untranscendent ("rasping", "tight"), yet so weirdly moving, it is easy to see why *News for the Ear* contains tributes not only from those one might expect – Gael Turnbull, Lee Harwood, Ric Caddel – but also such mainstream contemporaries as Thom Gunn, Elaine Feinstein and Fleur Adcock. In this sense, like the Kerrigan-Robinson book, it forces us to rethink notions about the boundaries between concepts such as "mainstream" and "experimental", which isn't to wish them away, of course. Fisher's droll account of the tribulations of gigging at The Crevasse Club, where the fourteen year-old Steve Winwood was his stand-in, would alone make this volume worth having; but it also serves as a perfect complement to the criticism by revealing the zest behind the poems. The last word on these books (and Fisher's own) is perhaps best left to Robert Sheppard, the joint editor of both: "These works cannot be written of (or even off) as minor or capricious productions... However much these texts dissolve poetic conventions, they are to be judged as poetry, and only by extending the paradigm of what it is possible to call poetry; that is their greatest distinction and their greatest challenge".

A Time Before Footwear

by Julia Copus

OWEN SHEERS

The Blue Book

Seren, £6.95,
ISBN 1 85411 277 5

JOANNE LIMBURG

Femenismo

Bloodaxe, £6.95,
ISBN 1 85224 540 9

ANDREW WATERHOUSE

In

The Rialto, £7.95,
ISBN 0 9527444 1 4

WINNER OF THE Vogue Talent Contest for Young Writers, shortlisted for a Forward Prize, photographed in *The Times* by David Bailey alongside Andrew Motion (by whom, incidentally, he was tutored at UEA), 26-year-old Owen Sheers describes his own work as "accessible and strong in narrative". *The Blue Book* contains tales about the exploits of larger-than-life characters in Fiji (where Sheers was born) and idyllic farm life in rural Wales; of stomach-turning adolescent violence, and of love.

The poems are packed with exquisite observations: paired cherries like "marbles of blood wishboned together"; a girl clutching a hoard of just-picked conkers to her stomach "as if you had been stabbed, and were / bleeding conkers from the wound"; "the slow hatching / of the paper lampshade larvae"; "the sound of ice, creaking like a boat's rigging".

All wonderfully evocative. And yet here and there these pages throw off the unmistakable stench of the writing school. A significant number of the poems in the first third of the book end with a crystallising two-line image, often a simile: "like a child, stealing a taste of the cake / before it is served"; "like words from under a memory, / vowels from under a tongue" and so on. It's not that there is anything intrinsically wrong with the formula, but the effect of coming up against it in such quick succession is jarring. In the end, the poems become so stifled by technique that their impact is deadened: the quiet mountains and creaking ice of rural Wales are drowned out by the thump of that looked-for final image.

The music at work in these poems is assured and effortless and rarely falters, though Sheers seems less at home with formal metres. An elegy to his grandfather begins, fittingly, in iambic tetrameter, like the start of a kyrielle: "I sometimes wish that we had fought / and turned our backs before you died". But then the pattern breaks down into something looser, before being picked up again in a single line towards the end. The resulting rhythmic imbalance leaves you wondering whether the poem's sentiment (the containing of emotion) might not itself have been better contained by sustaining the metre of those opening lines.

These are minor criticisms, though, and ones which it is perhaps unfair to level at a first collection. So let me redress the balance by quoting the last part of 'The Fijian Lay Preacher', which shows Sheers at his youthful, incisive best:

He once showed me the marriage pools,
where your choice was made in the throw
of a stone.

Hit the water, you take her.
Hit the rock, you walk alone.
He laughed at the thought

of nervous men, standing on the edge,
sweating into the pebble they held in their hand.

We looked a few moments more,
then walked on,
kicking the stones at our feet.

The Blue Book – now into its second print-run –
is an impressive debut, and Andrew Motion may
well be right in naming Sheers as a poet to watch in
the new millennium. If there's any truth in the
rumour that he already has a substantial body of
new work ready for print, it may not be long before
we find out.

Joanne Limburg

A mother who boils herself down for soup to feed
her family, long-dead relatives who turn up for
dinner, a chance meeting with Freud on a station
platform, the subject matter of *Femenismo* (also
shortlisted for a Forward Prize) is nothing if not
intriguing.

Limburg is currently studying for a PhD in
Psychoanalytic Studies, and she is at her best when
adopting various personas in an attempt to come to
terms with her own identity. Her amiable 'Inner
Bloke' is "a thwarted thug / and it's all thanks to
me, / the body he lives through, / my puny little
arms, / that girly way I kick". As the "Other
Woman" in 'Study in Watercolour', she becomes
"a charcoal mark, ingrained, / the one fixed point in
a landscape // that pours like rain through a gutter".
The imagery is well sustained:

I expect a storm and one appears:
a black cumulus in the shape of a wife.

I brace myself for a fist like a thunderclap

But too many of these poems end where they should
begin. Here's the last stanza of 'Wisdom at 3 a.m.':
"I can see a meaning in this weather, / if I look hard
enough – / a heavenly signature / left for excep-
tional people / like me, to read". Clearly she isn't
looking hard enough, as she never gets round to
sharing with us what that special meaning is. The
tone Limburg uses is often flat, the language loose
and prosaic: "They said it was boring, / the way I'd
always win. // They never knew / how hard I tried
to lose" ('Curse'). And the work is also marred by
technical weaknesses: there are some flaccid
rhythms and a number of decidedly dodgy line-
breaks ("I'm no / stranger to insomnia"; "she tells
me what / my problem is") whose placing seems
entirely arbitrary.

Happily, some of the natural cadences of speech
in 'Autodollography' are nearer the mark. In a similar vein to 'Inner Bloke', it charts Limburg's struggle with her own girliness, through her changing
attitudes towards the dolls she grew up with. After
five years of untroubled play, a family death
prompts the precocious infant to declare a "War on
all Dolls, / the snide, lying bitches, / with their
bodies with no openings" and "their mouths that
always smile", until finally she comes to a recognition that feminine charms have their uses; that
"dolls are perfect decoys" because they can "sit
cross-legged in pubs / laughing at other people's
jokes". There is a pleasing directness here, a sincer-
ity of tone, that lifts this poem above the mere
posturing of other, less successful pieces in the book.
Elsewhere, she seems content to let her doll-self do
the talking for her, presumably so that "No one
need ever know / what a nasty girl I am" – which is
a shame because, not surprisingly, the "nasty girl" is
a far more engaging character, and a better poet to
boot.

Andrew Waterhouse

Eight pages into this intoxicating collection (winner
of this year's Forward Prize for Best First
Collection) we come across the first poem of the
title sequence, 'In', which is picked up and contin-
ued every five or six pages throughout the book. It
is not clear from that first poem precisely where
"in" is, but that early ambiguity makes the rever-
beration all the more satisfying when the penny
finally drops into place. These are snapshots of life
as an in-patient at a hospital. The story ought to be
a sad one: the patient is apparently "in" for a depressive illness of sorts. Yet many of these short poems
are lit with humour. 'TV', a poem about watching
Star Trek in the patients' day-room, ends with
counsellor Troi, "beautiful, but surrounded",
reporting to the Captain:

"The aliens are angry, but mean us no harm. I
believe
we can help them." She is right and I am relieved,
nod my three heads, want to tell her everything.

The expansive feel of the book is due in part to
the vast landscapes – both natural and man-made,
ethereal and earthly, real and surreal – that exist

side by side in these pages, and in the poems them-selves. Waterhouse's topography teems with jungles, forests, moonscapes, cities, bars, houses, hospitals, coast-lines, industrial estates and ancient monuments. He has a way of bringing the natural world up close to us, pulling it into sharp focus, when we'd all but forgotten it was there. In 'The Need Fire', for instance, he entreats us to "Dowse the streetlights, the hand-held torches, the glow of the microwave. / Bring two logs from the forest behind / the supermarket".

Waterhouse's world is as mercurial as the care-fully chosen words with which it is conjured. Images of absorption and regression abound: we find "whirlpools eating themselves", explorers whose "extremities [are] reabsorbed", a butterfly "drinking its own wings", grasses "that yellow, withdraw roots", and "telephone lines [that] recoil to their source". And in 'Twenty (Including Double Word Score)' a couple "who may not be young but are hopeful" flirt across the unlikely arena of a scrab-ble board (like Ferdinand and Miranda at their chessboard), until "gently, but firmly // on the *o* of her *ovules* / he lays *throb,* leans close, / breathes: 'It could have been broth'". 'Errata' uses some subtle phonemic shifts to magic a series of noisome words into safer versions. "All ambiguity is constructive," he tells us: "*Harm* should read *home*", "*Fiends* should now be *friends*", "For *loathe* read *love*".

The intriguingly titled 'Why Our Sacred Tree Wears No Sandals and Why the Moon Sometimes Smiles' provides a useful insight into Waterhouse's very individual approach to the language of poetry itself. In a previous, human incarnation the Sacred Tree begins, after a Jesus-like spell of temptation and meditation on a mountainside, to describe to his people his vision of a time before man's supremacy over the world; a time when in fact we *were* the world:

> And after the saying of this, he took off
> his sandals, pushed his feet into the dry earth,
> until each toe extended, curled, became a root

Metaphor is the life-blood of these poems; and here as elsewhere it serves as the perfect vehicle for a process of integration, a dissolving of the bound-aries between the self and the outside world. It is no accident that there are a paltry two similes among the entire fifty-five pages of this collection. Waterhouse is simply not interested in comparisons and the diversions they effect; he keeps our gaze fixed firmly on the moment. And however bizarre his poems may be he persuades us, for the moment at least, that this is how things really are; he recon-nects us with "a time", as the Sacred Tree would have it, "before footwear / when we walked directly upon the earth". Amen to that.

Ghostly Comforters

By Steve Burt

PETER SCUPHAM

Nightwatch

Anvil, £7.95
ISBN 085646 3191

NIGHT WATCH IS Scupham's tenth book of verse, not counting a 1990 *Selected*; he published his first in 1972, when he was 40. His sensibility and tech-nique have always seemed deliberately, even culti-vatedly, behind his times. In his best work a tendency toward formal elaboration balanced an interest in other people's lives: some of that best work is new, and is here.

Scupham has worked before with whole books given to one project or theme: *The Air Show* (still his peak) consisted mostly of poems about his wartime childhood. Here the subject is old age, death, memorials, and ghosts, and the mood is resolved, civilized and sombre. The poems take place in a warm posthumous (sometimes, a post-imperial) 'Afterwards', an ongoing autumn where (as 'Night Kitchen' puts it) "Everything which happens happens in passing", "the chair sleeps in the clock's arms", and "the cats and spoons grow desolate and cosy". In rural France "the dead shut up shop these long afternoons, / careless of coarse marguerites, white cattle / dwindling to ghost-selves in the heat-haze…" In a dance tune the poet's mother enjoyed,

> The circling dog from HMV
> grows dark and gravelly as the sea

and every chord is asking where, oh where

are all those dancers who have danced off-screen,
the Bradford Pals, the shut-eye doll, the cat,
whose *Wanted* posters on the wall
say will-not-come when you-must-call,
however hard you beat the in-between.

Fancy and tawdry, high and low, all these gestures,
sounds and personages now seem equally precious,
because equally lost. The last third or so of the
book moves from such losses, through a delightful
if slight epithalamion, to a series of meditative
poems about history and the afterlife; several recre-
ate, in somewhat labored ways, Victorian scholars
and travelers.

Scupham's desire to commemorate fits naturally
with his liking for historical and familial subjects,
since history, genealogy and elegy all seek to bring
the past forward into the future, to show that nothing is completely lost. The four expansive stanzas of
'Family Reunion' imagines Scupham's deceased
parents dropping by his house:

They look as if they've chosen how to look,
deep in the prime of a late middle-age –
work to be done, but time for gardens, walks,
gadding off on some petty pilgrimage.
"Peter's books are so much neater than yours were,

John".
"That's because he never reads them".

This disturbing conversational slackness is one of
Scupham's several attempts to get some other tone
than the conventionally elegiac from the materials
of elegy. Another is the hushed astonishment of
'Parting':

You played in childhood at being dead
and look, it all came true,

learning to hold your breath for ever,
the bed singing itself out
to a drunk boat, a one man crew…

The central sequence 'Northern Line' merges
past, present and ghostly train trips around one
journey Scupham took at the end of a leave from
military service in the Fifties. Like most poems
about trains, this one emphasizes its passenger's
helplessness: Scupham's life (and modern English

history) seems to him a series of encounters he has
not chosen and could not keep. The reasonable,
muted, informed sadnesses are recognizably
Scupham's, though their lists, rhythms, and trans-
muted clichés owe something to MacNeice:

Back to the keys which wound the past too tight,
the fizz of clockwork, and the broken spring.
Back to the branch-line, Snelland, Wickenby,
the tired old brutes that clanked and puffed
before the Reverend Awdry got at them…

Troubles packed up in the old kit-bags
have drifted out through rusty eyelets
and cannot find their ghostly comforters…

The eleven-part poem (all in unrhymed pentameters) consists largely of impressions like these: some
are neatly made, but there's nothing to keep the
sequence (or any segment) from being half, or half
again, its length.

Scupham's best short poems are a different
matter. 'The Old Home' (an old-age home, of
course) shows Scupham's startling mastery of the
Hardy-Larkin method by which an entire sad short
story emerges from a stanzaic poem. 'A Trunk of
Letters' finds the perfect figure for its aged, redis-
covered correspondence:

This sea-chest disappoints: all cling-film faces
and little creepings underneath the skin,
brittle green ribbons and a black-head pin,
a night of family faces coming home

to roost, to babble volumes in, confess
how much they missed each other, what they read
in faces that were not yet photographs.

And the mysterious, beautiful 'Name and
Nature' takes its title and its donnée from
Housman's lecture 'The Name and Nature of
Poetry', which found the source of lyric in inartic-
ulate bodily distress:

O cry-for-help, caught between wind and water,
thing that would rather be said than be,
would like to die happy
out in the spell-bound garden,
covered all over in strawberry leaves

by an alphabet whirled in a puzzle of wind
which will not settle for anything less

than a cry for help
answered, as twenty-six letters
change each body terrestrial to one celestial...

The cry here is at once lament (as for the dead) and surprise (as at ghosts); it is, too, "the cry of its occasion, / Part of the res itself and not about it" (Stevens). A poem by Scupham (or by anyone) seeks not simply a commemoration but an addition to the world, something new and memorable.

With his fluently-managed stanzaic lyrics, his

casual, supple pentameters, his trains and old photos and National Service mementos, Scupham can seem defiantly unfashionable, or fuddy-duddy; he's neither a populist nor a great innovator, and he might not even mind being called Georgian. But this isn't a disadvantage, merely a mode, a name for the goals Scupham sets and the tools he has used. Humane, attractive and aurally deft, Scupham's best poems measure up to their models: they deserve more and closer attention than they have lately received.

TOM PAYNE
NOT EVEN ORPHEUS

On Leon Theremin, inventor of the Theremin (1897-1993)
after Horace, Odes I. 24

What is the right mood, the right seriousness
on losing one like you? The instrument
played with hands near, not on, with its wo-wo
       sings its most tearful song

now that eternal sleep has come upon
you, Leon Theremin. You'd known long sleeps
before, not only when the KGB
       snatched you away to doze

as if forever; also when a girl
lulled by that music box you worked – reworked –
died, you said, longing to recover her,
       "We must build a machine

to bring her back to life!" Your music worked
by letting go: two oscillating tubes
within a wooden case enabled you
       to pull sounds from the air,

the very air. How could bare hands refine
that atmosphere, and make it fit for lungs
music never sustained? Patience is all.
       Some things you can't put right.

KATE RHODES
TO DAMIEN HIRST'S SHARK

Unrepentant, honest,
With its Peter Benchley sneer,
Your face is always
A killer's face.

Your eyes snap shut on me
Pin hole small,
Obscenely focused.
No wonder they model cars on you,

Your striated gills are sleek by design.
From this distance you could strike me,
A muscled fist
In a tight leather glove.

When I lived in Winter Park
You were still alive.
The radio spat out the truth about you,
That boy on Vero Beach was eight, maybe nine,

They found his torn shoulders
On Merritt Island,
Then a few days later,
His head.

After that, for months
You inspected me coolly
Through the shark cage
Of my nightmares.

Smiling your fixed grin
You always found me,
Your keen fins cut
The pattern of my fears.

You prove we can't sell
Our ogres to Saatchi and Saatchi,
They still catch us in the shallows
At night, by stealth.

But now you're blind in a caustic sea
We swarm on you,
A gawping school of piranhas,
We pick you over.

Pickled in your stinging bath,
Your punishment is vicious,
Your sharpest tooth is just a charm now
To hang around a surfer's neck.

PETER BLAND
SHOPPING WITH BRIGITTE BARDOT

Naturally one remembers you as you were. At
your best, I'd guess, in *Viva Maria*,
singing rebel songs and letting off bombs
in a Mexican bar with some footlights on
and lots of revolutionaries cheering. Footlights
suited you – Louis Malle knew that –
and frills and corsets and torn Edwardian knickers.
What we wouldn't have given, back in the 60's,
to share your bed... if only for a minute!
Now you're into dogs and stray goats
because "they're always there" and "they never cheat me",
not like those playboys in the bad old days
who whisked you away, knowing time was short
and that what they craved
could only be borrowed. Today
you've put on weight, got some wrinkles
round the eyes and throat, but it's still a pleasure
to carry your dog food back to the car,
admiring your stride, feeling
nostalgically voyeuristic. There's
the scent of Chanel and warm milk on your skin
and when you get home the dogs start barking,
eager – like the playboys – to get you to themselves,
to lick you to death and cover you in kisses.

RUTH FAINLIGHT
THE MECHANISM

Jump off the memory-go-round
whose jangling roar and varnished glare
jolt you awake

Veer out of the path of those plunging
creatures with flaring scarlet nostrils
vacant insect gaze

The whirling sheets of printed paper
rhetoric and propaganda
blown into your face

A desecrated dream-world, gone
from pastoral to derelict
to post-disaster waste

Then force yourself back on and seize
the lever of the mechanism.
Now hard-brake.

HELEN OSWALD
NIGHT FLIGHT

At the airport your lips pull
duty free on a fag. Resolve slips.

Tonight touch shocks, returns
everything lost. Love burns.

In sleep you cross into bilingual dreams –
you have more homes than one it seems.

You show up quarterly on the phone bill –
my voice has entered unseen cities at will.

You and I exist in flight
between arrival and departure and delight.

STEVE ELLIS
STAINTONDALE

If I painted this, it would be this alone:
a mellow brick ramp, buried in growth
of flowers and wildness. But poetry says,
"Evoke the gentleman ghosts of yesteryear
lighting a pipe, checking the clock;
have them drift among these briars now.
Chubby shop-girls, maybe a mother
with a boat-size pram, the station-master
with his watch-chain and couchant dog,
set in an aureole of brass and blacking,
liveried in chocolate-brown paint".

And I reply, bugger the age of steam.
This is no scene for its sooty nostalgia
but this thought alone: that someone,
for the sheer love of composition,
and all the beauty of brickwork,
should build eight feet of useless wall
shaped in a wedge, cope it with stone
and plunge it into a pile of colour:
baked earth, floral earth, sunning itself here,
and every shade of burnished red
and every nuance of moss and mortar.

ROBERT SAXTON
TOKYO

Such tricky steps precede the normal fling!
That nurse you might have admired
    has an x-ray
      of your heart and a soft spot, it's said,
      for a sumo welder.

They lie on their backs at cherry viewing,
their sensibilities inspired
    by *ukiyo-e*,
      the floating world of the almost-wed,
      while the earth turns colder.

Those who twirl and those who cling,
the cool and the wired,
    abuzz with the hearsay
    of blood, mooch at the fountain-bed,
    waltz like Matilda.

City without love, there's no such thing.
Our people get so tired
    at the end of the day
    many passengers fall asleep with their head
    on a stranger's shoulder.

CATHERINE FISHER
FOLKLORE

Beyond the forest lies the mountain
made of glass; no doubt you'll have to climb it,
slithering, fingers and palms sliced open,
on the far side see the lake through your pain.
You'll need a boat, and there may be a fee;
some object picked up on the way,
a comb, a crown. A lot to pay.
Or some impossible task, a million seeds
to be gathered, a forest to cut down
or dragon's teeth to sow; that means
you'll need a helper, wise and shrewd, some
beast that talks.
        And deep in the dark blue water
there'll certainly be a fish with a ring
in its belly, and you'll row with it in your blistered
hands to the island. Where you'll
find the tree, one tree always, that holds
up the world, that bears the perilous
fruit, and in its topmost branch will be
the nest. So you must climb, giddy
and swaying in the gale, between the dove
and the phoenix, and in the twigs
there'll be one egg. One golden egg.
You'll pick it up; it'll be frail, but you must
crush it. You must close your fist
and feel the warm yolk dripping from it.
Because this is my heart.
And you must break it.

FAY HART
YOU COULD HAVE ME FOR A DOLLAR

You could have me
for a dollar
spend me in a day
or in an hour
I could take you
to the cleaners
leave you
or call you back tonight
we could round up
guilty parties
make the whole damn thing
so festive
like a blessing in a church
or a wake
we could walk away tomorrow
hand in hand
with all our sorrow
and wind up on a beach
or in a park.

PHILIP GROSS
SINGULAR

for Zelie

Love, be flagrant and delicate,
a riot of tact, the careless falling-
into-place exactness of it all.
Be the singular coupling, the lingering
lightning strike, the solemn giggle
loud-hushed, through the midnight wall.

Be the tink! of ice cubes on the edge
of melting in an equatorial heat;
the sun, downed in one gulp, pops up
to a raucous creche of parakeet

and howler monkey: ancient cries,
today's news in the forest canopy,
same difference, the first time again. Us?
I-and-I, as Rastas say. That singularity.

JOHN KINSELLA
IL FAUT CULTIVER NOTRE JARDIN

Cleared land is a place of weeds,
bee-wings' razored whirr
and a cut trunk hollowed
by white ants – a font
beneath swabs of cloud.

When sunlight cordons
off an area for display,
hill-clefts and ravines
resist, retaining shadow.
Small birds sing and you

don't think of their name,
the air-drag of crows' wings
just overhead. Jam
trees keep their sap
tight beneath the bark.

Late winter warmth
dries cushions of moss,
rapidly brittle and crumbling
around purple sprays
of Paterson's Curse;

onion grass cuts low weather
and twenty-eights are caught
in a pause, a cessation
of dialogue – instruments
poised about the developing fruits

of the creek canopy.
Working their tails, chests
puffed and springing angles
like hearts, claws hooked
as numbers in a code

that won't quite scan:
but neither does god!
A globe-bodied spider
concentrates a poison
that bothers only flies,

mosquitoes and ants;
the sun intensifies and parrots
are burnt to silhouettes,
a clear night with frost threatens,
plants folding like prayer.

PATIENCE AGBABI
SUN, SNAKE, WINGS

For Alan, Lal and Naresh

The first time I flew too close to the sun
before I could claim it with graffiti,
a single ray pitched its sharp solar flag
in my right shoulder. For three months it burned
charcoal black till I found it a lover,

the same one who twisted his two-forked tongue
round Eve's little finger. My left shoulder
mummified. Itched. Shed its skin. And I woke
next to my past life, cracked as old leather.
For seven long years, a seven-year itch

tortured my spine, a constant reminder.
I grew wings, red-black feathers and flew so
close to the sun, the sun was my mirror.
Then I turned my back. And it was just like
the first time. Sharp, intense and forever.

Hungary's Secrets

by George Szirtes

ATTILA JÓZSEF

The Iron Blue Vault

Translated by Zsuzsanna Ozsváth and Frederick Turner
Bloodaxe, £8.95
ISBN 1 85224 5034

THE TWENTIETH CENTURY has been a remarkable one for Hungarian poetry. If only the rest of the world knew it! But there are merely ten million speakers of the language inside the country and, owing to border adjustments and diaspora at various times, some five million abroad. The language is isolated, difficult and, however beautiful it can sound, it looks daunting. It has been said that the late Sandor Weöres was up for the Nobel Prize ten times but the translations available couldn't do justice to him. "It'll have to be our closely guarded secret", shrugged a rueful Hungarian editor. And so many secrets: from Lörincz Szabó, Arpád Tóth, Lajos Kassák, Dezső Kosztolányi and Mihály Babits through Miklós Radnóti, István Vas, Gyula Illyés, János Pilinszky, László Nagy, Agnes Nemes Nagy, Ferenc Juhász and Weöres himself – which is not to mention those still living and those I haven't mentioned for fear of making the list too long – the very names seem destined to be hidden. And there is Attila József who was born in Budapest in 1905.

Often, it seems, the fascination of the life itself can create interest in a poet the West – especially the vast sprawling territories where English of one sort or another is king – might otherwise ignore: Radnóti's body discovered in a ditch with his finest last poems in the pocket; József's birth into desperate poverty, his struggles with Marxism and psychoanalysis, and his suicide in front of a train in 1937, have a dramatic validatory power. I can hear voices, excitable, mythopoeic voices exulting: "No middle class examination of one's own belly-fluff for these guys! How different from the home life of our own dear Mr Bleaney". No one wants the natural fouled-up kind of guys. And this too is sad, as sad as those other poetic martyrologies from Keats, through Dickinson and Plath. The drama is in the poems not in what lies outside them.

However! József's mother, Borbála, was a washer-woman whose husband deserted her with several children ("What a giant was my mother," exclaimed József in one of his best loved verses, 'Mama'). She slept together with four of them on a single mattress in the basement of a slum. It was impossible. A foster mother was found who took the children into the country, where József worked as a swineherd and was regularly beaten by his foster father. After a couple of years Borbála, came back for them but József ran away from her and pulled a knife on his sister. Borbála was suicidal. At nine years old József too attempted suicide.

Life was never easy for József, a small, handsome, potentially delinquent boy. Borbála died when he was fourteen. At this point an improvement in his circumstances through some respectable relatives meant he was able to attend school again. And he began writing poetry. Having written a love poem thought to be dedicated to the principal's daughter a scandal broke about him and he attempted suicide again. He survived once more, and this time as a poet. He published his first volume in 1922 when he was seventeen and it found support, but he was having to take menial jobs. Things never did run smooth and sometimes they ran very rough indeed.

The rest of the history is given in detail by Zsuzsanna Ozsváth in her part of the introduction to her collaboration with the American poet Frederick Turner in their translation of some of József's poems, *The Iron-Blue Vault*. The life, in this case, is so much a fabric of the poems that there is no question of special pleading. I don't think it means that we should be reading the poems to discover more of the biography, but that the biography supplies the character and very essence of the poems. József's enormous power lies in harnessing both the diction and the hunger of a street kid with a desperately hopeful romantic and political vision. And, of course, a remarkable lyrical gift. Although he was adopted and then cast out by the communists, after his death he was raised to exemplary status by them and his raw energy has exerted enormous, if indirect, influence on much Hungarian poetry. For a non-Hungarian reader I would suggest imagining a cross between an urban industrial John Clare, a less dreamy Robert Desnos, the boy Rimbaud, the middle to late Dylan Thomas and, just possibly, the Douglas Dunn of the *Barbarians* period. If you have got this combination right you should be feeling a little giddy, but that's the right frame of mind for József. There are a few versions available but the current book, the work of Edwin

Morgan and, earlier, of Vernon Watkins, seem to me to represent the best of his work.

The Iron-Blue Vault is strongest on the Desnos /Thomas side, in that it goes for richness and formal virtuosity, which it achieves more often than it has a right to. One of the major poems, 'On the Edge of the City', begins, in English:

> Where I live on the edge of the city,
> behold as dusk caves in
> like bats on insubstantial membranes
> the soft soot glide and spin
> and settle, as the layers of guano do
> in a thick, horny skin.

Apart from "behold" and the slightly coy "guano" this has the swing, scope and physicality of József, and that is a real achievement. That the translations of many of the poems maintain this level is something to be grateful for.

But – and this sounds like carping but I believe it's true – József outruns them as he has outrun all the other translators so far. Nevertheless, I recommend *The Iron-Blue Vault* as a way in, for the biographical material, and for glimpses of the man. Edwin Morgan has, I think, got closest to the heart of the poems. Check out his *Collected Translations*, itself an exemplary volume.

Prophets of Rebuke

By Jonathan Treitel

A Hundred Years of Modern Hebrew Poetry Found in Translation

Translated by Robert Friend
Edited and introduced by Gabriel Levin

Menard Press, £9.99
ISBN 1 874320 23 3

Songs from Bialik
Selected Poems of Hayim Nahman Bialik

edited and translated from the Hebrew by Atar Hadari
with an introduction by Dan Miron

Syracuse University Press, £16.95
ISBN 0 8156 0605 2

THE HISTORY OF Zionism is the history of the modern Hebrew language. At every stage in the endeavour to create a Jewish national identity, the language in which to express it had to be invented. The Hebrew poet, then, is at the creative centre of Zionism.

The poet who is usually regarded as the father of modern Hebrew poetry is Hayim Nahman Bialik, who lived mostly in Russia, and who wrote in the late nineteenth, early twentieth century. In Israel

today, he is famous – every schoolchild is made to read him – but he is seldom appreciated. For one thing, his Hebrew is quite different from that spoken on the streets; in particular he used the Ashkenazi accent, in which the word-stress is utterly unlike that in Israeli Hebrew, so his metrical patterns are inaudible to the modern reader. Also, his romanticism belongs in a faraway era.

In a new translation, Atar Hadari aims to make Bialik come alive. As he concedes in his preface, his poems are versions rather than literal translations. He often ignores the original metre and rhyme; he follows the broad sweep of Bialik's metaphors, but does not seek to communicate the author's precise intention. I found this effective: Bialik comes across as a readable, powerful, supremely ambitious poet, who combines the personal and the political.

The poem that launched Bialik, 'City Of The Killings' is a response to the terrible pogrom in Kishinev in 1903. It begins:

> Rise and go to the town of the killings and you'll
> come to the yards
> and with your own eye and your own hand feel the
> fence
> and on the trees and on the stones and on the plaster
> of the walls
> the congealed blood and hardened brains of the dead

The poet goes on to berate his fellow Jews for letting themselve be oppressed; but not without holding out some hope. To quote from another of his poems, 'The Legend':

I understand finally that though this race is worms
it will yet cope with and bring down giants.

Bialik, then, was in the tradition of the Biblical
Prophets of Rebuke – and indeed his Hebrew
alluded to that – but what made him accessible was
that the author did not separate himself from those
he was rebuking: he too was a suffering worm with
noble aspirations. He wrote poems about nature,
his parents, his sexual fantasies... and created a
persona many Jews then identified with. He
emigrated to Palestine in his later years and wrote
very little there. When he died in 1934 it was a
national day of mourning – it is said that a hundred
thousand (half the entire Jewish population of
Palestine then) attended his funeral.

In Hadari's versions, Bialik comes across as
rather modernist. For example, take the final stanza
of the poem 'Summer Is Waning'

And the heart is orphaned. Soon a cloudy day
will knock at the window in the silence:
"Have you checked your shoes? Mended your coat?
Go out and prepare the roast potatoes".

Compare the version of this stanza in *A Hundred
Years Of Hebrew Poetry* translated by Robert Friend:

The heart is orphaned. Soon
the cold rains will be drumming.
"Have you patched your coat for winter?
Stocked potatoes against its coming?"

All of the nine Bialik poems selected by Friend
are personal rather than political – reading these
alone, one would get a distorted impression of the
poet. Contrary to what one might imagine from the
title, this volume is not an anthology of somebody's
idea of the best poems from the most important
Hebrew poets. Robert Friend was an eccentric
fixture on the Jerusalem literary scene for decades.

An American Jew who spoke poor Hebrew, he
wrote his own, rather precious, poems in English;
he translated Hebrew poetry persistently but dilet-
tantishly. After his recent death, this book was
compiled as a tribute – it gives one a stronger sense
of the translator than of the translatees. He was
limited in his sympathies: he had difficulty with
both polemic and overt political statement.
Rhythmically, he liked to make the flow manage-
able, dividing it into bite-size pieces; he sometimes
strained too hard for effect; he was never convinc-
ingly slangy. He was at his best only when he found
a poem which corresponded to his own tastes.

Take, for example, the opening stanza of a poem
by Yehuda Amichai:

My father fought their war four years or so,
and did not hate or love his enemies.
Already he was forming me, I know,
daily, out of his tranquilities.

The superfluous "or so" and "I know" – the unnatural "tranquilities" – all for the sake of getting the
damn thing to rhyme!

Notwithstanding, this collection does contain
fine translations of numerous excellent poems,
many of which were new to me. There is much to
give pleasure here. Uri Zvi Greenberg's 'The Hour
Is Tired ...' is a prime example:

The hour is tired as if it were time for bed;
and like a foundling in a white nightshirt only,
I sit and write in the void as if upon a blackboard:
nothing matters, nothing matters.

If the black cat should leap among the platters, lap up
what's left of the white milk, and overturn the platters,
I'd close my eyes for sleep, I'd sleep forever –
nothing matters, nothing matters.

Spring issue – Seven Years On

The **New Generation Poets** promotion in May 1994 signalled both the arrival of a new
wave of poets and the beginning of a concerted effort to raise poetry's public profile.
Seven Years On looks at the progress made by the poets since (including those influential poets who fell the wrong side of the age cut-off point) and effectively consti-
tutes a Who's Who of the contemporary British poetry scene.

Grim Didactic Ground

by Carmine Starnino

EAVAN BOLAND

The Lost World

W. W. Norton, $21.00
ISBN 039304663X

THROUGHOUT HER CAREER Eavan Boland's self-pleasuring ear has always needed to bargain with themes so politically preemptory – the stereotypes of women in Irish myths, the suppressive conventions of traditional Irish poetry, her own bardic striving for imaginative room in a paternal literary canon – that they risked running her whimsy down to grim didactic ground. In writing the poems for *The Lost Land*, however, Boland has ruinously opted to cut a deal on some very unfavourable terms. Reminiscent of Adrienne Rich's recent propagandic efforts, Boland's new collection finds its ardour not in spry articulateness but in short-winded truisms. The verbal stretch that gave a poem like 'Outside History' its adventuring thrill has been clipped by a party-platform sensibility. Boland, in other words, is now a poet with a sermon. Of course, it's too early to diagnose whether she's lost the negotiatory knack that previously helped safeguard her aural gusto from the forthright political character of her topics. Truth be told, poets as gifted as Boland don't usually write this soberly unless they really want to. And what we seem to have is a poet who no longer wants to be vigourous but wants to be venerable:

> I put my words between them
> and the silence
> the failing light has consigned them to:
>
> I also am a daughter of the colony.

> I share their broken speech, their other-whereness.
>
> No testament or craft of mine can hide
> our presence
> on the distaff side of history.

The cosy imperiousness of "them", "their" and "our" is evidence of how Boland has enshrined herself as Official Custodian of Female Irish History. What's saddening (speaking as a fan) is that the exciting stylistic crisis of Boland's feminist daring – "the fission of music into syllabic heat" as she once memorably put it in 'The Women' – has been snuffed out by the marmoreal coolness of a public voice. To put it another way, if these poems rarely feel formidable, it's not due to any missing seriousness. We are disaffected because there's no play to Boland's purpose. A pleasing line or two sometimes tempers her flat-lining utterances – "the faraway, / filtered-out glitter of the Pacific" or "one house with its window, making / an oblong of wheat out of light" – but Boland is no longer game for any adjectival capering. (The collection takes so many long pensive walks that I longed for some of the frivolity that Medbh McGuckian's or Carol Ann Duffy's or Kathleen Jamie's poems splash in.) I can't even declare the writing grandiose because even gradiosity requires a kind of annunciatory stride. Instead, there's now a vacant elegance – by which I mean that if her lines have a lapidary quality it's only because she's put nothing interesting in them:

> I have two daughters.
>
> They are all I ever wanted from the earth.
>
> Or almost all.
>
> I also wanted one piece of ground:
>
> One city trapped by hills. One urban river.
> An island in its element.

So I could say mine. My own.
And mean it.

I wish I could assure you that this sample is unrepresentative, but everywhere in *The Lost Land* we encounter poems foiled by facile thinking – matters are either too briskly explained or vaguely confronted. The fault, of course, lies with Boland so hawkishly eyeing the General Truth that her poems are denied the latitude to independently pursue their own felicities. The risk this poses to her writing is considerable since any idiom left neglected for too long faces almost certain exhaus-

tion. And indeed one of Boland's more pronounced stylistic tics is her habit of tapping out lines using a paratactic stutter: "Arms wide. Lips apart. Last words."; "Their faces. Arms. Greatcoats. And tears."; "Ireland. Absence. Daughter."; "To this. To us. To earth."; "Seeds. Raindrops. / Chips of frost". The fact that this sort of melodramatic stop-and-go comprises the most effortful moments in this collection is itself a mortifying indication of the woodenness Boland has now claimed as a right. She seems either to have forgotten what it takes to escape the doldrums of typical poetic stances, or (more likely) thinks it not worth her trouble to do it. Am I wrong to presume that readers deserve better?

Presences

by Jem Poster

ANNE STEVENSON

Granny Scarecrow

Bloodaxe, £7.95
ISBN 1 85224 534 4

ANNE STEVENSON ONCE said that each of her collections to date represented a fresh chapter in her poetic development. *Granny Scarecrow*, her first new collection for seven years and her first with Bloodaxe, suggests no radical change of direction; but the mood is more distinctly autumnal than in her 1993 collection, the tone more deeply elegiac. Friends have died, ways of life changed, and it's not surprising that a number of these poems should register lost connections. In the title-poem a dead woman's print dress, attached to a wooden cross to scare birds, functions as a shadowy after-image of the woman herself, giving her a continuing – though gradually diminishing – footing in the lives of her two granddaughters and blurring the line between presence and absence; but the two girls mature and die in a very different world:

Marjorie, divorced, rose high in the catering profession.
 Emily had children and grandchildren, though,
 with the farm sold, none found a cross to fit their
                                                clothes when
 Emily and Marjorie died.

As even this poem shows, however, and as others demonstrate still more emphatically, Stevenson's visions of loss are importantly counterweighted by an awareness of continuity. 'Comet', an elegy for the Welsh historian, Lewis Lloyd, juxtaposes references to the visitation of the Hale-Bopp comet with unsettling intimations of mortality, concluding with a composite image simultaneously suggestive of persistence and impermanence:

There, blazing back of my eyelids, comets' tails,
indelible Vs grooved in salt water by wrecked prows.

Burned into the retina or mind, imprinted on the landscape or on the page itself, the dead claim an afterlife not in some separate sphere but among the living upon whose breath, as Stevenson memorably puts it, "the past depends". The subject of one elegy is "up and among us, free, smiling at everyone", while in another a faintly irritable Ted Hughes interrupts the poet as she embarks on her tribute to him, explicitly resisting commemoration but actually stamping his presence firmly upon her text. The poem she had intended to write would have emphasised absence – "you've flown away now" – but Hughes' disapproving shade will have none of that. "Please don't imagine", he corrects her, "I have / flown anywhere"; and the words which conclude the poem are, significantly, not Stevenson's own, but those of Hughes and his implacable roosting hawk: "I'm going to keep things like this".

There are other ghostly voices echoing through the collection. In 'John Keats, 1821-1950' Stevenson makes explicit the idea of her subject's afterlife, as a "spirit... come back, in me, to Michigan". And not just to Michigan, in 1950: half a century on, Keats' sallows, crickets and wailful gnats find their place in a new poem which delicately acknowledges the continuing presence of the past, both as personal recollection and as cultural inheritance.

The finest of these poems work, with a visionary fluency reminiscent of Woolf, towards a freedom from conventional chronology. In 'An Angel' the speaker contemplates "a black hole of infinitely compressed time", experiencing a "blink into genesis" and a rapid "fast-forward" before emerging from her vision to find herself not, as she had thought – and told us – on her bed in Wales, but still apparently travelling towards her destination; and these dizzying temporal slippages find subtler correspondences in such poems as 'The White Room', 'Going Back' and the superb 'Arioso Dolente'. In each of these Stevenson reaches back into a past already pregnant with a future now known to her, traversing family history with an ease

which might be described as playful if her disclosures were not so chilling. The poet's grandmother, standing on the threshold of marriage, casts a shadow which seems, from her perspective, to represent a bridge to a promising future, while her granddaughter, with the knowledge granted by hindsight, sees it extending through "money-troubles, / syphilis and silence" to "the bride-white room we had to visit / with its incense of Bible-leather, / mothballs and sweet unappeasable hurt". Or, still more poignantly, Stevenson revisits a younger self who sits at the piano playing Beethoven to a father blissfully unaware of his daughter's future deafness. "What happened", she says, "is what the living teach the dead"; and the lessons can seem almost unbearably hard. There's grief here, certainly, but very little nostalgia or regret. It's in the nature of Stevenson's poetry to honour the past without diminishing the present; and if the collection is in part a lament for vanished lives and worlds, it's also a demonstration of continuing intellectual and imaginative vigour on the part of the poet herself.

Talking Heads

by Sarah Wardle

CONNIE BENSLEY
The Back and the Front of It
Bloodaxe £7.95
ISBN 1 85224 518 2

THE TITLE POEM of Connie Bensley's latest collection pictures a couple who view life differently. The woman sees only surface glamour in a restaurant, or a circus ring, while the man prefers to go into the kitchens, or backstage, to witness real life. Like Jack Sprat and his wife, between them they see *The Back And The Front Of It*. Bensley herself is like the man, observing people and places with a sharp, cynical eye. At the end of the poem she predicts that the pair's relationship is doomed and wonders: "which / will be the first to stray?" This is the six million dollar question, and she borrows from Larkin, a fellow cynic, adapting the close of 'Days':

This is the question
which brings the clowns running,
with their jibes, their pointing fingers.

His influence is also felt in 'Friend': "Larkin was right: however we may grieve, / we know that what survives of us is love". Arguably, Bensley's realism and concern with a suburban landscape ally her with a Movement line.

She is a deft satirist and mistress of characterisation. Many of her poems read like *Talking Heads* sketches: a cab driver praises his second wife, a social-climbing mother despairs of her drop-out son, a man fantasises about his cleaning woman, a wife is annoyed at how her husband and sister get on. Even Jesus makes an appearance as a man in a pub, marvelling at the miracle of a headline about a heart transplant. Sometimes her scenes are more solemn and set in the past, as with the patient in a Fifties sanatorium, or the girl evacuee who experiences menarche without her mother nearby. 'Getting Out of Hand' depicts a ghostly, literary tea party, with a cast, including Rupert Brooke, Jane Austen and George Bernard Shaw, calling out to be filmed by Merchant Ivory. Many of her pieces could be transferred to the screen. In 'Leviathan' something in the body politic of suburbia grows like a triffid, or alien. 'Mésalliance' is like a Roald Dahl tale, where a woman wants to divorce her dog, or failing that murder and bury him. 'Time to Part' and 'Reunion' are cinematic sketches where ex-lovers meet, but do not connect.

She is not shy of turning the camera on herself, either to send herself up, as where she likens herself to the spinster poets, Emily Dickinson and Stevie Smith, or to record her bleaker moments. In 'At Madame Tussaud's' we are left guessing whether the narrator, who has had an affair with a famous person and encounters his waxwork image, is in fact the author. She chronicles the joys and sadness of affairs, grandchildren, insomnia and ageing. In 'Birth Day' she describes her daughter giving birth, while she herself waits by the phone, feeling powerless to help, as "Time stops". In 'Holding Hands in the Movie Show' she pictures herself at sixteen, squeezing hands with a boyfriend at the movies, then fast forwards "half a century later" to a grandchild clutching her hand as they watch a horror film. Instead of the ubiquitous thirty-something single, she is part of the sixty-something generation, who has been through the mill of marriage, children and divorce. Rich experience of life mixed

with a sharp intelligence is the recipe for her satirical sense and darker observations.

However, after reading the collection I was left wanting something more. In *The Name and Nature of Poetry* Housman defined poetry as something more elevated than wit. Whilst I would disagree with him and argue that wit and satire have their place, I found myself wanting more of a balance than Bensley provides. She has a talent for form, but I wanted her to apply it to haunting, Longleyesque lyrics, as well as to satirical verse. I would also have liked her occasionally to venture beyond the end of the District Line. A moment of epiphany comes to her whilst eating an ice cream, when out shopping. A man, who has at last forgotten his ex, stands at his bedroom window marvelling at oleander buds in his garden. These are both valid moments of connection, but surely she could get closer to nature? Similarly, she could mine deeper veins of thought, or float away on higher ideas. She has perfected comedy and satire, and can handle serious matters with deceptive ease. But I would like to see her extend her repertoire and be more geographically and theoretically adventurous. Her observant eye examines "the back and the front of it", but she sometimes stops short of exploring above and below and peering inside.

Vamp, Now Ready

By Phil Ramage

KIT WRIGHT

Hoping It Might Be So

Leviathan, £10
ISBN 1903563 01 1

HOPING IT MIGHT BE SO collects thirty-six of Kit Wright's new poems together with his adult poetry spanning the last twenty-six years. This collection clearly illustrates the quality of Wright's work. Presented in a reverse chronological order you get the new poems under the *Hoping It Might Be So* banner at the beginning of the book, sliding back eleven years to the previous collection *Short Afternoons*, then back another six to *Bump Starting The Hearse*, six again to *The Bear Looked Over The*

Mountain, then to his contributions three years earlier in *Treble Poets*. Kit Wright's adult collections have hardly been regular – eleven years has been a long time to wait. But the poems on offer here suggest that the wait has certainly been worth it.

Wright's poetry for children is evident in almost every primary classroom. His poetry is enjoyed by everybody from the most able to the most reluctant reader. There can be few children who have not at some time in their school career handled a copy of Wright's work and experienced the vibrancy and humour of it. In my teaching career I went through a number of copies of his two most renowned collections, *Hot Dog* (1981) and *Cat Among The Pigeons* (1987) – either these books were made of flimsy materials or became dog-eared because of the amount of use they got and I know which reason I favour. Many of the children who laughed along with *Hot Dog* would have now reached adulthood, and, on rediscovering Wright, will find so much that they relished in his children's poetry evident in his work for adults. Wright should be as well known amongst the general adult population as he is with the youngsters.

If you read the book from back to front (but why would you do this? It is obvious that we are meant to read it from the newer poems first) you can appreciate the development of the voice and the skill of the poet. Right from the 1974 collection the sheer talent is there (I love 'Berkhamstead Castle' – an example of a not very exciting tourist spot) but it seems to me it is from the *Bump Starting the Hearse* collection that Wright is firing on all cylinders. It is here that the technical skill, the sense of fun, the confident coming together of form and content really shows that the earlier potential was being realised. Even more impressive is the range of the poet's work. Poems which stand out from this collection include the stunning indictment of cricket's involvement in South Africa during apartheid in the chilling 'I Found South African Breweries Most Hospitable', the hilarious 'Personal Advertisement' with its repeated refrain of "Bloke Needs Poke / Send Pics / Box 6" and the wonderful 'Like A Fairy Tale', a bizarre short story in five verses about the winner of the Senior Personal Freshness Challenge Bowl – the deodorant as the saviour of modern society!

'Frankie and Johnny in 1955' is a sparkling achievement. Not being around at the time, my knowledge of the Ruth Ellis murder trial is largely restricted to the 1985 film *Dance with A Stranger* directed by Mike Newell and yet I got a stronger feel for the story and the time in which it was set from reading Wright's thirty-four rhyming couplets than I did from watching Miranda Richardson and Rupert Everett do their stuff. This is achieved with some wonderfully daring lines which rhyme "trousseau" with "to do so", "ox-eyed" with "perox-ide" and he brings the whole thing crashing down to earth with the final bathetic couplet:

Or how they could hang you on a Holloway hanging tree,
Poor little Ruth Ellis, two months before ITV

'The Losing of Liverpool' borders upon the epic, yet remains rooted within its very Englishness, with the dockland streets of Liverpool and the Mersey at its centre. Within its seven quite bleak sections we meet the freezing and "past it" prostitutes plying their trade to the "exceedingly sleazy geezers", together with the eccentric Joseph Williamson, "the mole of Mason Street", who dug his way under the

streets. Images of neglect and decay pervade this poem. It is many miles away from the sanitised freshness of 'Like A Fairy Tale'.

On the back of the book the publishers describe the new poems as "dazzling" and this is very apt. I would defy anyone not to be dazzled by the range and quality of these new poems. 'Beryl's Dad Comes Clean' sees a much under-rated children's comic character, Beryl the Peril's dad, come to life "all kniving knees and elbows" – Wright only too happy to illustrate that the child Wright is still lurking within the adult form and the end result is delightful, right to the menacing conclusion where

…it gets darker
out in the garden behind the house
as the blood drains from my suit.

That marvellous sense of fun is present in the wordplay of 'The Orbison Consolation' where Roy Orbison's most famous lyric (I won't need to tell you which one) is questioned with a range of similar rhymes that may have even tickled the morose Mr Orbison himself. The beautifully nostalgic 'Mantles' throws light upon a childhood memory of a grandmother's house where the lamps "were taught to flower in the dusk". In complete contrast, thematically, the image of those living rough in Camden Town in the powerful 'Beggars' will remain long after the poem has been read.

Hoping It Might Be So is evidence that Kit Wright is one of the finest and liveliest poets writing today. Here is a writer very confident with form and rhyme, and even though there are recurrent themes (the elderly, the eccentric, cricket – all very English themes with Wright having something to say about that in 'Everyone Hates The English'), the range of content is breath-taking. Wright may come closer to laying his cards on the table about his poetry in the poem called 'Poetry':

I like what vamped me
In my youth:
Tune, argument,
Colour, truth.

There is much to "vamp" the reader in this collection. It is clear that Kit Wright is neither sandwich-board carrier nor prostitute (his suggestions, in the introductory 'Something About the Author') but is one very gifted poet. This is an essential purchase.

No Room for the Rondeau

By David Wheatley

The Making of a Poem:
A Norton Anthology of Poetic Forms

Ed. Eavan Boland and Mark Strand

Norton, £19.95

ISBN 0393 149167

IN HER POEM 'Formal Feeling', Eavan Boland recounts the classical tale of Cupid's encounter with Psyche. Always visiting under cover of darkness, he flees in alarm one night when Psyche lights a lamp. Cupid considers his form as something above such petty scrutiny, and is distraught at the woman's getting to see "the place where the sinew of his wings / touched the heat of his skin / and flight was brought down – / To this. To us. To earth". For much of its history, the mystique surrounding literary form has scarcely been less intense.

Contemporary poets don't think very much about form, critics are often heard to grumble. But no less a problem is the (self-contradictory) tendency to think of the subject in abstract terms. The worse excesses of this can be seen in the largely mundane and formally unexciting work assembled in the New Formalist anthology *Rebel Angels*. Boland and Mark Strand wisely avoid the polemics of *Rebel Angels* in *The Making of a Poem*, their anthology of formal, if not formalist poetry. "The charm and power of poetic form", we read in the 'Overview', is that "it is not imposed; it is rooted", a statement Boland and Strand illustrate by rooting their introductions squarely in autobiography. Strand remembers his adolescent wonderment at Archibald MacLeish's 'You, Andrew Marvell'; in a memoir of her college days Boland recalls the "hard and bleak" quality of terms like iamb and trochee. If writers begin by treating poetry as a sort of school bus on which they hitch a ride, the great step forward for Strand and Boland came when they rolled up their sleeves and got under the bonnet of some poems of their own.

The Making of a Poem is designed as a hands-on affair, taking its complex forms out of the metric museum and putting them back in an easily graspable context. Thus, it reminds us that villanelle comes from Italian *villano*, "a peasant", and may have its origins in country round songs sung with refrains, and illustrates the sestina with a repetitive conversation about whether or not someone has been to the store (perhaps Jerry, Kramer and George talk in sestinas on *Seinfeld*?). It offers bullet-pointed sections like 'The Sonnet at a Glance', with pedagogic directness overruling scholarly nuance (are there really only "two kinds of sonnet"?). A handful of poems are selected for "close-up" treatment, though it's difficult to get too close to anything in the half-page to which Boland and Strand restrict themselves.

Since *The Making of a Poem* is properly international in scope, it's a pleasant surprise to see writers not often mixed in together sharing anthology space: Les Murray side by side with Lucy Brock-Broido, Mary Oliver with Medbh McGuckian, Gjertrud Schnackenberg with Thomas Kinsella, Babette Deutsch with Francis Ledwidge. Best of the book's twelve sections are those on elegy and pastoral, among whose contemporary poets are Frank Bidart ('To the Dead'), Douglas Crase ('The Elegy for New York'), Alfred Corn ('A Walrus Tusk from Alaska'), and Robert Hass:

> There are moments when the body is as numinous
> as words, days that are the good flesh continuing.
> Such tenderness, those afternoons and evenings,
> saying blackberry, blackberry, blackberry.
> ('Meditation at Lagunitas')

Nevertheless, something fundamental about *The Making of a Poem* failed to click for me. Here are many indisputably great poems, by Chaucer, Spenser, Shakespeare, Milton, Dryden, Pope, Wordsworth, Tennyson, Eliot, Auden, Heaney and others, yet the anthology struggles and fails to live up to its subtitle. The list of things you won't find here is not just surprisingly but startlingly long for a book that boasts of "sections devoted to all the major forms": among them are Skeltonics, the ghazal, terza rima, the rondeau, the ballade, acrostics, the alexandrine, concrete poetry, octosyllabics, the fourteener, rhopalic verse, the clerihew, to go no further. The haiku, that staple of even the most formally challenged creative writing workshop, doesn't make it into the glossary. An even better-known form, the limerick, is nowhere in sight either. The ballad qualifies as one of the "major forms", but the epic, the monologue and the verse letter do not. I don't expect Strand and Boland to print a couple of epics just to keep their bases covered, but some explanation is needed; none is forthcoming. What are they up to?

It's difficult to say. *The Making of a Poem* does not eschew literary history, but tends to present it in a tone somewhere between blandness and apology. If something doesn't fit, it is simply shunted aside. Strand and Boland don't consider the tradition of classical quantitative metres in English worth a single mention, from Sir Philip Sidney to Robert Bridges and Peter Reading, one of the most formally accomplished writers in English today. We do get told about the existence of accentual verse, in a very brief glossary, but aren't treated to any examples of pre-Chaucerian English poetry. British poetry seems a particular blind spot: a section on elegy that blithely ignores Geoffrey Hill isn't going to convince too many, and the omission of one of the most formally conscious poets of the century, Basil Bunting, is simply impossible to understand.

Even without any engagement with the classical tradition, *The Making of a Poem* is not any more informative on non-Graeco-Roman forms. Where are writers like Austin Clarke, Hugh MacDiarmid, or David Jones who have learned from non-English language forms other than the holy trinity of sonnet, villanelle and sestina? Yet again, not in these pages. The university creative writing market was presumably on Norton's minds when they commissioned this book, but it doesn't have much going for it as a reference tool. Readers with the curiosity to go further might have been told about Saintsbury's *A History of English Prosody* or the *Princeton Encyclopaedia of Poetry and Poetics*, but a very skimpy "Further Reading" section doesn't stretch that far. On the gender question, no one will object to correcting the male bias of previous anthologists, but when we find makeweight poems by Lucille Clifton, Carolyn Forché and Ai bizarrely sharing a section on "Open Forms" with 'The Love Song of J. Alfred Prufrock' and 'The Circus Animals' Desertion' (open form?!) we have entered the realm of very special pleading indeed. Nor are safely canonical women writers much better served. Marianne Moore is here in a section on odes, but no mention is made of her masterly achievements with syllabics.

In his poem 'On Teaching the Young', included in a section on the stanza, Yvor Winters writes: "The poet's only bliss / Is in cold certitude – / Laurel, archaic, rude". It doesn't take cold certitude to sense that were he around today that sternest of critics would have some rude things to say about this book. It isn't only poems that need form: anthologies do too, and on that count *The Making of a Poem* reads like a hasty first draft.

Acutest at Its Vanishing

by Justin Quinn

MICHAEL PALMER

The Lion Bridge: Selected Poems 1972-1995

Carcanet, £12.95
ISBN 1 85754 442 0

MICHAEL PALMER IS one of the few L=A=N=G=U=A=G=E writers who have found enthusiastic readers outside experimental enclaves like Haight-Ashbury and Buffalo. The testimonials come in fast and thick even from poets who appear regularly in a mainstream outlet like the *New Yorker*. It is difficult to say why. There might be a tokenist element to these endorsements: poets who receive a generous cheque for appearing in a glossy middle-brow magazine could be worried about appearing too square to appreciate what's going on in the margins. More seriously, it could have something to do with the fact that Palmer, for all the disjunctions and non-sequitors, has maintained some connections with the lyric tradition. On the most superficial of levels, his poems don't look experimental in the least: there are couplets, stanzas, blocks of conventional-looking free verse, the odd piece of prose. On another level – I had wanted to say "thematic level", but that's another story – the reader encounters more or less lyrical descriptions of landscapes and atmospheres; there are even some poems addressed to his daughter and some responding to the Gulf War. In the matter of tone, it is cool, steady, calm, and more or less unchanged over the twenty-three years covered in *The Lion Bridge*; it is a voice somewhat reminiscent of Hal in *2001*. A poet such as Susan Howe at least holds out spars to the reader in the form of lucid prose prefaces to her poems which provide the information necessary for connecting her work with Swift, Melville or the Defenestration of Prague. These at least are something to grab onto when the maelstrom is swinging you about.

And what a maelstrom. Palmer's work had been recommended to me by many writers and critics whose opinion I value, so I was favourably disposed to the poetry beforehand. But after two tours of duty through its 250 pages, I retreated baffled and fatigued. I discovered when turning to read more accessible work by other poets that my eyes just scanned down through the lines without registering the thread of what was being said. What's it like? Here are two verses from 'Lens':

> I failed to draw a map and you followed it perfectly
> because the word for "cannot" inscribes itself here
> to define an atmosphere of absolute trust
> which both fastens and unfastens us.

> The branches of the pine drooped heavily
> in the moist air and this was pleasant
> though at times it felt a little unpleasant
> that he couldn't balance on his head

Perhaps the tone is too even to call this a maelstrom, but it not meant to be understood in any conventional way (one section of an early book is entitled 'The Book Against Understanding'). Take for instance the first three lines of the second verse: as almost everywhere else in the book where Palmer is conventionally descriptive, it is not clear if the reader is to imagine this scene has something to with the reported events in the previous verse (a coulisse or setting for them?), or whether we should view them as an example of the kind of "language counter" we use when we talk or write. It seems, although I can't be completely sure, that Palmer drifts between these two modes, often expatiating for a good few lines on a particular scene, only then to step back from it abruptly into meta-linguistic awareness with another non-sequitor, though what governs these transitions or what is meant by them

is obscure.

Sometimes that awareness of the mechanisms of language, that plastic sense of language's doings, results in startling passages. This is from the first poem in the book:

> To begin, "the stamp"
> of autumn... these parades
> whose curved names
> folded in as pilgrims.
> You start to swim
> through a little darkness
> and see some trees

The names, the words, stream out like parades, like pilgrims to name the transformation of autumn, and that motion is like that of the self out of darkness into the daylight of reality, borne by language. Maybe I'm imposing narrative where none was meant, but subsequent poems in the same collection would seem to confirm the reading. Sense here is just within reach, and for that the writing is acute; but when it vanishes completely we are left floating through line after meaningless line. Nothing is subverted, not bourgeois syntax, not flows of capital, not economies of desire: there is only boredom.

Sure I was missing everything while reading *The Lion Bridge*, I felt sorely in need of an intelligent and insightful exposition of Palmer's work to help me find a way in. Difficult poetry always needs such advocacy in the beginning. I remain hopeful that illumination will come, but it had better be an improvement on the advocacy this work has received in the US for the last while. Time and time again critics like Marjorie Perloff, Hank Lazer and Michael Davidson will quote a block of L=A=N=G=U=A=G=E poetry and append the same kind of comment, i.e., this poetry "resists those (paternal?) codes that enforce coherence in favor of exploration of other modes of thinking" (Lazer on Charles Bernstein). Those modes are never specified, but those paternal codes – let's drop the question-mark – are bashed *ad nauseam*. L=A=N=G=U=A=G=E writing now needs the kind of critics who will explain what the poetry is gesturing *towards*, and not for the hundredth time saying-what it's *against*. Anyone who cares about poetry will always be interested in any movement that extends the possibilities of the art; the antennae should remain up and functioning, and in the case of Michael Palmer the field is wide open to anyone who would try.

Some More of the Old

by John Whitworth

VERNON SCANNELL

Feminine Endings

Enitharmon, £8.95
ISBN 1 900564 076

Views and Distances

Enitharmon, £7.95
ISBN 1 9005 6425 4

SCANNELL'S NOVEL FITS snugly into a genre, which, so far as I know, contains just three examples. There is Dylan Thomas's notorious collaboration with John Davenport, *The Death of the King's Canary* (i.e. the Murder of the Laureate), which remained, Ulysses-like, unpublished for years because of its libellous remarks about Thomas's contemporaries. There is an unpublished masterwork of my own where one of the participants on an Arvon-type course kills a course leader. And there is what we have here.

I am sorry Scannell did not see fit to kill off ghastly Gabriella ("call me Gaby" – presumably pronounced Gabby), a member of the Society for Cutting Up Men who ought to have been gagged with her own awful poems and forced to listen to a thousand lines of Kipling. Instead she wins a big prize and finds true love. But in spite of my disappointment that the only murder turns out to be a red herring, I enjoyed this book and read it right through in one day, an unusual thing for me these days.

The plot is slight. There are three sexual couplings, male-homo, female-homo and hetero, rather better than par for the Arvon-type course, I would have thought. Arvon and Tŷ Newydd courses I have attended were more remarkable for the alcoholic rather than sexual excesses – but perhaps I had no idea what was going on. Scannell has some difficulty in differentiating all the characters; there are twelve participants, two poets, two people running the venue and a mad gardener, who must be drawn from life because he has no place in the plot, and this is too many for a novel of less than two hundred pages. But Scannell has an agreeable

style (something else we know from his poems) and the novel bowls along with a following wind of interesting talk, rather in the manner of the works of Thomas Love Peacock which I occasionally dip into (and so should you if you don't already).

Satirical targets are not too hard to identify. A pop poet called Brian Macduff (Brian Patten + Roger McGough) and a feminist poet called Melissa Hull who has written a book called *T-bone Psalms* (Selima Hill, who wrote *A Little Book of Meat*, and also, perhaps, her brother-under-the-skin Geoffrey who wrote *Mercian Hymns*) are not present in person which is perhaps just as well or Scannell's book would have suffered the fate of Thomas/Davenport's. But they are brooding presences, salient examples of WHAT IS WRONG WITH THIS PICTURE in the poetry scene nowadays. In other words Scannell has parodied them, amusingly if pretty broadly. There is also hairy nature poet (who?) and a rather good parody of Sylvia Plath's overpraised (according to me) 'Daddy' called, wait for it, 'Mummy'. A fair amount of what I take to be Scannell's own poetic views are put forward by his mouthpiece Gordon Napier, an old and bibulous poet who once won prizes but doesn't even get published nowadays (unlike Scannell) because of the likes of MacDuff, the Nature boy, Gaby and Melissa, of whose combined *oeuvres* he thinks not a lot. Is he any good, this Napier? Oh I think so, judging from the examples of his work we see. Frankly I think he would have little trouble getting published – perhaps he doesn't try very hard. Though of course Roy Fuller did have trouble placing his last book – a scandalous state of affairs surely.

The Scannell/Napier view of poetry is certainly OK with me, though I can't quite forgive Napier for reading the *Guardian* at an age when he should know better. Or is that Scannell being satirical, even satirising himself? I do think he's unfair to Roger McGough, a subtle and interesting poet who has suffered, not so much from success (I should be so lucky) as from being corralled with Patten and Henry, pleasant but definitely lesser lights. And though I don't understand Selima Hill either, she certainly has a magical way with words (better than Scannell gives her credit for) even if it's emphatically not my way. No, if I were writing the book and putting the boot in, then it would be... er a bunch of other poets entirely.

In general, of course, I am sympathetic to all old-curmudgeon-type views – I would be, wouldn't I?

Napier's teaching goes quite well and though one student leaves in a huff it isn't his fault. I remember that happened to us in Tŷ Newydd (the reasons were different). At least no one puts poison into the Spaghetti Bolognese, as I was reliably informed happened elsewhere once. The fellow confessed before anyone had taken a fatal spoonful and roamed the hillside all night, wailing in an agony of contrition. No real poison in Scannell and the parodic poison is fairly genial. Much better than Thomas/Davenport's (which is rather boring actually) and to be recommended. As are his poems, just what you would expect from Scannell and no nonsense about development here. "For God's sake, give me some more of the old!" I cry like Doctor Jekyll, and that. God be praised, is exactly what I get. I like them all and I know a lot of other people who will like them, in particular an ex merchant seaman at a class of mine who started writing poetry in his sixties; I shall give him the copy the Editor sent me – because I have the book already, you see;

I am a Scannell fan. 'Word Games' is a fine illustration both of how to manage trochaic tetrameter and of why we should bother to do so. 'Overheard in the Student Bar' is funny and all too true. And in 'Poet Tree' a Midland boy who has previously heard the word as "poitry" is momentarily thrown by his Southern schoolteacher's pronunciation. Then he understands – actually misunderstands – but his misunderstanding is true and poetically fruitful:

> Suddenly he saw the marvellous thing
> Quite plain in silvery sunlight, tall, serene
> Against blue sky, its branches blossoming
> In multicoloured vocables, from green
> Syllabic buds, the flowering Poet Tree,
> Where for centuries fabled birds had sung,
> And under whose protecting canopy
> Poets had dreamed, or from its branches swung.

Scannell just goes on getting better.

JULIA COPUS
IN DEFENCE OF ADULTERY

We don't fall in love: it rises through us
the way that certain music does –
whether a symphony or ballad –
and it is sepia-coloured,
like tea that stains as it creeps up
the tiny tube-like gaps inside
a cube of sugar lying by a cup.
Yes, love's like that: just when we least
needed or expected it
a part of us dips into it
by chance or mishap and it seeps
through our capillaries, it clings

inside the chambers of the heart
to atriums and ventricles. We're
victims, we say: merely vessels
drinking the vanilla scent
of this one's skin, the lustre
of another's blue eyes skilfully
darkened with bistre. And whatever
damage might result we're not
to blame for it: love is an autocrat
and won't be disobeyed.
Sometimes we almost manage
to convince ourselves of that.

Jesus in Jeans

by Greg Partridge

EDWIN MORGAN

New Selected Poems

Carcanet, £7.95
ISBN 185754 4595

A.D.
A Trilogy of Plays on the Life of Jesus

Carcanet, £14.95
ISBN 185754 4986

It's artistic
To have ordered impulses. To
think the world has makes you feel great.

Beyond the world, the slow-dying sun
flares out a signal fan, projecting
a million-mile arm in skinny hydrogen

to flutter it at our annals.
Coarse, knee-deep in years, we
go on counting, miss the vast unreason.

(from 'The World')

NOT EVERY POET composes vigorously circumspect poems titled so vastly as that, but very few poets seem to be at home in as many wildly, juncturally-coloured strata as Edwin Morgan. Not just in present day Glasgow, where he is the city's first ever "poet laureate", but St. Andrews (for Milton's boyhood) and Venice (for Stravinsky's funeral) and Paris (for Rameses II's final exhumation); not to mention Jack London's digs in heaven and Lord Jim's ghost's favorite haunt. From microscopic intimacy, to a pinhead sized Earth – how does Edwin Morgan get around so well?

No one could miss how supremely mobile his imagination is, confident that all can become a shared space if one only bothers to investigate. Nor could one accuse him of a lack of variety. This volume of *New Selected Poems* offers love poems, humorous poems, experimental poems, sonnets and narrative verse. Morgan's many books have included works of familiar formal structures to prosy story telling and free verse, and the present collection offers all of these in chronological order.

The *New Selected Poems* begins with several poems that feel like agglomerations of all the various faces of his poetic expression, especially some "shaped" poems that "be" more than they "mean", with text artfully smeared and streaked across the page. These poems provide as good an introduction as any as to how Morgan goes about conferring poetic creation on his subject material, those things that he chooses to treat as readily plausible and poetically useful, rather than persuasively dispossessing them of phenomenality.

These shape poems are inventive, but not always what some of us would consider genuine poetry. Perhaps the experiment-inclined Morgan would point out that this is asking "capital P" poetry to fulfill its own recipe even when that variety of poetry isn't incarnate in the composition at hand. Still, 'Archives', 'Opening Cage', and the much anthologized 'Computer's First Christmas Card' are enjoyably diverting, putting on ironic exhibit some of the noodling that goes with verbal exploration. Likewise, some of the prosy humorous pieces, such as 'The Mummy', are genuinely funny and entertainingly realized.

Morgan also has powerful stories to tell, little verse dramas like 'Stobhill' of the *From Glasgow to Saturn* volume. Characters are sketched in their own glib and familiar words, surprised that such an incident (a foetus not yet deceased is discovered in a trash bag after an abortion) could happen to them, could occur at all. And the first person poems comprising the sequence 'Planet Wave', composed for musical accompaniment, likewise sketch hovering consciences, even in surroundings dating as early as twenty billion B.C.

All of which is to say that whatever the preferences and tastes peculiar to an individual reader, successes abound in this collection. Other than a few occasions when Morgan submits to the temptation of editorializing (such as 'Urban Gunfire' or 'The Flowers of Scotland'), the often unpleasant or politically charged subject matter of much of his work actually reveals Morgan to be wonderfully free of sanctimony, never imposing himself as a hero of regret or condolence upon his subjects. And still other poems, like 'Cinquevalli', thrill with a simplicity and brio found in few contemporary poets' work.

For this reader there remain a few baffling poems, like 'What is *Paradise Lost* really about?', which did not suggest an answer or illuminate the question. Others, such as 'Vico's Song' (recalling the earlier 'Opening the Cage') twist along on syntactical imbrication, as if to reproduce the residual effects of grammatical parsing. The lines are purposefully run-on, the meaning perhaps crotched between, or to be found in the turning over – but maybe too glibly, in the absence of bigger ideas:

the universe that turned in on itself
turned in on itself
on itself
self was
was the universe
that was turned in
it was the universe that was turned in

'Floating off to Timor' might be a good representative of Morgan's lyrics that are devoted to love and desire. In it the speaker admits that desire is something divisible but which takes dominion in divided places. Rather than personally talking up such frustrations into poetry, Morgan has desire take up dreams, specifically the replacement of the lover's familiarity through a regretful fantasy of escape, "those desires we keep for strangers".

Perhaps a useful way of exploring elements of Morgan's poetry, his choosing of subject and that subject's eventual representation via his voice, would be to stretch his gift of voice – lending it to actual, unfolding dramatic situations. And in fact Morgan has made an ambitious exploration of dramatic representation, in a new trilogy of plays entitled *A.D.*, written in his prosiest manner but with lines carefully demarcated by breaks that help direct spoken performance.

The plot is of course largely familiar from the Gospels, but if you experienced or endured a religiously connoted secondary education, you might also be very familiar with the typical illustrative "Bible sketch". In Morgan's trilogy, the hint of a school play is not unwelcome, as he gives us a contemporary Jesus in flannel shirt and jeans, capable and healthily masculine though not averse to talking like his counterpart in the Gospels. Other elements of this drama also have familiar raiment, including some rebellious young Jews, with rebel anthems and rebel salutes; a Joseph who tries to think for all his family via a fusty patriarchy stretched too tightly; and an older brother for Jesus named Jude, who is impatient with the various desert preachers' self-importance that makes the public washing away of small-beer sins a full-time preoccupation.

This Jesus is a stern critic of his oppressors' fetish-making of symbols of their own power; he refuses to repair a statue of Jupiter for his employer and despises a Caesar who has not earned what is supposedly "his". Heathen gods (declares Jesus), belong in libraries accumulating dust. Importantly, he helps build a theatre in the party-town of Sepphoris, a wealthy and exciting city with amenities reminiscent of modern Amsterdam, in which dildos and wrestling make an appearance (as they do in the Old Testament) and where Jesus finds

that Sophocles' martyred Antigone has made upon him – she a persona of conviction as real to Jesus as his lover Helen (the woman with whom he fathers a child):

What is there in a play that can do this?
I am so ignorant. I am shown up.
In the midst of life I find myself in art.
In the midst of art I find myself in life.

The striking thing about A.D. is how much Morgan's real-time theatrical art tends to work like his narrative verse, even though the stakes seem higher. Ingeniously he uses the make-believe world made available by the existing biblical setting to put the hard questions of narrative coexistence and endurance to passive spectators – putting his audience into the shoes of Jesus by having him also experience a play: "O she is real! Not more than Helen is real, / But real too in her own word-given way.

Jesus finds he must try to understand how reality could be "word-given" in both theatre and politics, even if his own certitude is endowed by God. This is not merely Jesus' drama; it is his audience's drama, one made plausible by this being an actual play but made from a familiar story. And affecting, too, because Jesus' only life must, and really should never have to, take the painful course for which it is always headed.

Factory Life

By Tom Fulton

FRED VOSS

Carnegie Hall with Tin Walls

Bloodaxe, £8.95
ISBN 1 85224 473 9

FRED VOSS IS a machinist who writes poems, and *Carnegie Hall with Tin Walls* is a collection of his best work. Most of the poems are vivid vignettes of factory life, but they are also much more. They comprise a wide-ranging social-political commentary that exposes the raw, concrete realities of class conflict, racial tension, and social injustice. The poems also deal knowingly with male woundedness, insecurity, alcoholism, grief, and shame. In a handful of self-revealing poems, Voss speaks eloquently of the reciprocally redemptive nature of art and physical work. In the middle section of the book, there is a cluster of poems that move outside the tin walls and speak to the pain of poverty in the lives of marginalized people everywhere, particularly the homeless. In all the poems, there is an earthy compassion that reflects a true spirituality.

The Goodstone Aircraft Company is an amalgam of the factories in which Voss has worked. It's an environment where the machinists bring their internal demons into an inferno of stress. They endure a stream of disrespect from powers farther up the hierarchy. The poems report the many indignities of corporate hypocrisy along with the wide variation of responses; the men behave in ways that are crude, offensive, cruel, infantile, yet sometimes inspired and creatively playful. Disrespect and its consequences is a recurrent theme of the poems, which tell tale after tale of small, carefully observed, day-to-day tragedies.

For Voss, the factory is a claustrophobic world of barely suppressed rage, impotence, and pained stoicism — a toxic environment, both literally and emotionally for the workers, who he sees as "outcasts who somehow managed to carry the world on their shoulders". Above all else, *Carnegie Hall with Tin Walls* can stand on its descriptive merits alone, without any social, political, or psychological interpretation. Voss gives us a stream of images recording the horrors and lunacy of the shop floor, from severed fingers to environmental hazards ('Eyes Open'), the ever present din of "roaring noise and pounding shockwaves" ('Tenderized'), the strains of working second and third shifts ('Shifting Lives') and the greatest horror of all – layoffs ('Broken' and 'Doing Time'). Yet amidst this chaos, there is still the dignity, the poetry, the music of craftsmanship as in the title poem 'Carnegie Hall with Tin Walls':

> ... from brute force
> to the most delicate touch on earth,
> they have played their bodies
> like virtuosos
> play pianos.

Amidst his straightforward accounts of existential futility, Voss presents sensitive stories that illuminate the grim essence of underlying social issues. 'It's Okay', 'Old Souls', 'Round 15' is a trio of poems that together constitute a profound essay on racial tensions. Voss is particularly good at candidly portraying the troubling of issues of sexism. He reports the machinists' sexual aggression in cringe-inducing bluntness, while also observing the insecurity and wounded longing beneath it, as in these lines from two contrasting poems:

> Whenever a good-looking secretary walks down the
> aisle...
> the machinists make a point of staring at her...
> Finally, when it is safe to quit whistling and moaning
> tributes to her body,
> they return to their machines,
> reassured that they have once again passed the test.
>
> ('The Inspection')

Just
a click clack of a secretary's high heels
across the concrete factory floor just
a scent of her perfume in the steel dust air...
may be enough to make the difference between life
and death.

('Lifesavers')

Voss's poems of men and women, particularly 'Aircraft Factory Love' and 'The Gesture', stand out as precise, perceptive tales of universal romantic and desperation. All of Voss's poetry seems suffused with grief and loss in its many forms, including the insurmountable emotional barriers among men, beautifully sketched in this excerpt from the poem 'Something None of Us Ever Talked About':

For five minutes or so some mornings
as we stood on the cold concrete steel mill floor...
All the machines
and the crane chains so absolutely still...
we might almost have begun really talking to each
                                                    other
for the first time,
so quiet
we might even have begun to tell each other
our dreams...

The theme of grief also occurs in a variety of poems that describe in human terms the impact of the computerization of the industrial environment and the accompanying dislocation and erosion of pride. The workers with whom Voss feels the most kinship are those from foreign countries who are still in touch with a tradition of craftsmanship in industrial labor.

Voss's poems of factory life are complemented with personal poems, which reveal his own complexity. Voss's feelings about his fellow workers' lives are elusive because he allows his multitudes within to freely voice their contradictions. Sometimes he seems like a voyeur, detached, even alienated from those around him. Other times he seems deeply connected by love and admiration. These apparent contradictions, within reveal the soulful essence of the plural psyche, occur also when Voss talks about the meaning of his work both as poet and machinist. In his most personal poems, Voss repeatedly returns to the themes of survival and precarious salvation. In 'Alchemy,' he describes

himself as a man whose life was saved by poetry:

Art can be made out of
the beautiful girl
who took every ounce of my heart away with her...
And I don't think
I would be alive today
if it couldn't.

In 'Life Raft' he is a man who survives through his work at the machines. Yet in other poems he seems to experience the factory as a trap.

I was particularly moved and impressed by those poems at the midpoint of the book in which Voss leaves the factory to explore the stark pain of poverty with stunning insight and compassion. These poems, which include 'Community', 'Intellectuals', 'Bared Souls' and 'Waste', are all the more effective because they bypass political abstractions and instead provide compelling images that move the heart – images of people "without one dream left to light their lives". It takes courage to write with unapologetic compassion in an age of irony. Voss is especially good when writing about homelessness, as in the poems 'Disowned' and 'I Know This Man', which addresses the subject with a simple, direct spiritual consciousness:

In the alley
I meet him:
a man who has had his humanity stripped from
                                                    him...
the finest most brilliant arguments in the world
will never convince me that he deserves to be there
for he is me
if I had not somehow stumbled across that job
it was the luckiest day of my life
to find.

Voss's poems relentlessly expose the soul-deadness that rests beneath the surfaces and denial of modern culture. In this sense, I found they moved my imagination in ways that seemed to go beyond their content and even beyond their depth of emotion to something archetypal, perhaps to the wounded, lame, neglected Greek god Haephestus, craftsman god of the forge, betrayed again and again by his wife Aphrodite. But that would be another review.

The Geoffrey Dearmer Prize

MAURA DOOLEY ON THIS YEAR'S WINNER OF THE GEOFFREY DEARMER PRIZE: **ANNA WIGLEY**

ANNA WIGLEY

WHEN I AGREED to judge the Geoffrey Dearmer Prize I had no idea I would find it as difficult as it proved to be. These poets, each with a manuscript ready to be a book, struck me as inventive, capable, memorable and durable and each was wildly different from the next. All of these poets were ready to publish *first* collections and the poet who has reached this point of expectation and fulfilment will never again face a moment quite like it. All of a poet's life up till then is poured into the shape of that first book. So I was lucky enough to be reading a group of rich, intelligent, imaginative poems by a group of talented writers whose first collections will be well worth waiting for. Anna Wigley brings a crystalline gaze to bear on the natural world. Her best poems detail, in a sophisticated but probably unfashionable way, the changing light on landscape, the movement of the seasons, the particular habits of particular birds. All these things are summoned with a sharpness of language, with vivid and passionate images which linger in the mind and through this carefully delineated world she shows us the bigger picture.

TWO POEMS BY ANNA WIGLEY
MOSS

I had never seen the colour green
until the Long Mynd moss
lay at my feet in a cold rain,
burning;

as if some temperamental goddess
had turned out her jewel-box
here, on this stubbled heath

then set fire to the lot.
And this was what was left:

the just-cooling embers and coals
still on their necklace-strings,
curling like miniature constellations
in a fern-and-heather heaven.

BELOVED DAUGHTER

The crows that perch on her stone
are older than she was.
Their caws go over
her scant twenty inches.

What would she have made
of this maze of graves?
She would have recognised silence,
rain, gently amniotic,
and tiny muffled thuds.

And the air would have stirred
some memory of being wheeled,
just once, outdoors.

But greenness and birds,
and trees like living houses,
and the sky(not even handled
with a word)

– these she now lies under
like her last home,
though she did not stay
long enough to meet them,
and knew neither feather nor stone.

NEWS/COMMENT

RAINEY DAYS

Poetry, ostensibly a liberal art, is actually one of the strongest remaining bastions of pre-literate tribalism. Gangs form as readily as in any deprived ghetto and the patterns of bonding rituals, territorial marking, hysterical crowd behaviour, collective log-rolling and hatchet-work, are worth the attention of the anthropologists. The occasion for these musings is a the sight of the pack turning on one-time *capo* Craig Raine.

Raine has presented a huge target recently, with his new magazine *Areté,* book-length poem *A La Recherche du Temps Perdu, Collected Poems*, and a new collection of literary essays, *In Defence of T. S. Eliot*. Many, it seems, have been lying in wait for just such an opportunity. The books were reviewed by the novelist Rachel Cusk in the *Evening Standard* (6 November, 2000) in a piece so vituperative one wonders what on earth Raine can ever have done to her: "the over loud tones of someone used to a captive audience", "brings to mind the contents of a schoolboy's diary", "dwelling incessantly on body hair, on orifices". The piece was headed 'Look at me, I'm a Poet'. Michael Hofmann in the *Observer* (3 December) wasn't much kinder – "pomposity and cleverness in smelly socks" – but what was most striking about the piece was the way it was presented: the title was 'Raine, Raine go away', and it was flagged on the cover of the *Review* section: "He thought he was a contender".

The viciousness of these attacks can be ascribed partly to the store of irritation Raine has built up over the years by his ostentatious declarations that he is the T. S. Eliot *de nos jours*. The charges against him are just and much of his recent work has been simply ridiculous as we pointed out, re *A La Recherche* and *Areté*, in Endstops, Vol 89 No 4, p.94). But for many years Raine could apparently do no wrong: Michael Hofmann was happy to be published by him and Rachel Cusk kept her peace. This open season for Craig Raine baiting clearly has little to do with literature but a great deal to do with the English class system, the politics of Oxford University and the aforementioned literary tribalism. The hysterical adulation that greeted Raine twenty years ago ("It is not fair that one man should have such inexhaustible brilliance" – Laurence Lerner) and the chorus of abuse he is now receiving are both perversions of good literary practice. Is it too much to hope that poetry will one day be beyond all this fiddle or must it always remain a swill-tub of the baser emotions?

WILLIAM SCAMMELL 1939–2000

As we were about to go to press I heard of the sudden death of William Scammell. Besides his other accomplishments as poet, critic, editor, Bill Scammell was *Poetry Review*'s lead reviewer from my first issue in Autumn 1986 until...when? Impossible to say, exactly. The idea of a lead reviewer is entirely unofficial and notional but at any one time there seems to a reviewer with more appetite and bite than the others, and for a few years it was Scammell. I'd admired his pieces in *London Magazine* so he was a natural recruit.

Scammell's early death and his difficulties in his last years bring home again the perilous nature of a poetic career: what so often begins in gladness is more likely to end in despondency and madness than in a Heaneyesqe glow of wealth and praise. His son Ben's obituary in the *Independent* refers to his problems in finding a publisher in later years and his disenchantment with the periodicals to which he had often contributed, including, one must assume, *Poetry Review*.

It had been so different in the '80s. He was a late starter in poetry, having left school early. Education – English and philosophy at Bristol – came after a succession of unskilled jobs. His unusual background for a poet stood him in good stead. His love of literature was all the deeper through having been gained through years of very unliterary work.

His first book, *Yes & No* (Peterloo, 1979), seemed to me one of the best of its time and announced the arrival of a poet who could marry demotic energy to learned wit. Peterloo collections came thick and fast in the '80s and early '90s. In 1989 he won the National Poetry Competition and the collection that followed, *Bleeding Heart Yard* (Peterloo, 1992), is probably his best. He was a great Dylan fan and his lines about Dylan "on kissing terms with art and kitsch" could be a motto for his own poetry. He like the cultural stew, the adulterous *mélange* of everything. The exuberance of his best work was infectious:

And sweets came of the ration
And jazz sprang up in dives
And Comets screamed on newsreels
And Woodbines came in 5s.

In his last book, *All Set to Fall off the Edge of the World* (Flambard), his long years in Cumbria finally produced a nature poet. In 'The Shearing' sheep are seen as a symbol of British resilience: "...each one as crotchety / and hard done by as / the British since the war".

In his reviews he was a ferocious enemy of cant. He had a boundless enthusiasm for poets such as Ted Hughes (whose prose he edited in *Winter Pollen*), Keith Douglas, Derek Mahon, and Seamus Heaney, but he was at his best as a reviewer when putting the boot in: "the...affliction of American poetry is inflation, wide-eyed syllabics, grandiosity with a capital Gosh"; "Tom Paulin has opinions the way Siva has arms – if his left doesn't get you the right probably will"; "The course of any and every communist takeover so far is as minutely predictable as the behaviour of a heated gas or the chord changes in a pop song". The pungency of this political *aperçu* is the key to one of his difficulties. Being pretty much an autodidact, he couldn't be doing with the strange tribal politics of English culture with its confusion of snobbery and insouciant sang-froid with oracular wisdom. His last piece for *Poetry Review* was a review of Christopher Rick's *The Oxford Book of English Verse* (Vol 89 No 4, p.45). Though relatively benign by Scammell's standards, this review showed his republican leanings aroused by Ricks's use of the handles *Sir* John Betjeman and *Sir* William Empson. It concluded: "The English genius for mixing up art, 'heritage', and flummery should be severely discouraged". Amen.

PETER FORBES

NET VERSE

Internet poetry expands at such a rate that Net Verse can only hope to pick out a few highlights. Sometimes important resources don't get a look in until after they're well established. One site you could argue I should have mentioned long ago is *Mudlark* at **http://www.unf.edu/mudlark/** This is a fine magazine, with each issue devoted to the work of one or two poets, giving each one a substantial airing. Back issues are maintained, so the site is building into a substantial library of work. Formatting is kept simple, so *Mudlark* is fast to load.

Another place I'm astonished to find I've not mentioned before is Tim Love's Literary Reference site at **http://www2.eng.cam.ac.uk/~tpl/lit.html** This is a vast and well-organised collection of links. Tim reckons that poetry about poetry is undeservedly frowned on, so is taking a stand against this with his new site Poetry about Poetry at **http://homepages.tesco.net/~magdtp/pap.html** He's seeking material for this, so if you've a self-referential poem you've not found a home for, you know where to send it.

K.M. Dersley has some fine poems, and essays on Bukowski and Kerouac, at his *Ragged Edge* site at **http://www.raggededge.btinternet.co.uk/** He's now started including guest poets, the first of which is jazz poet Gerald Locklin.

Seamus Heaney, Anthony Thwaite and Thom Gunn are just three of the poets interviewed at **http://www.interviews-with-poets.com/index.shtml** The site is promoting print versions, so you don't get everything here. Nevertheless, the extracts are generous and interesting, and well worth visiting.

If you want a bit of light relief after that, you could do a lot worse than drop into Adam Taylor's Poetry Place at **http://www.poetryplace.co.uk/** where you'll find some excellent humorous poetry, much of it with a sharp satirical bite, from this Yahoo UK Poet in Residence.

Let me know about other sites that deserve a mention, via **peter@hphoward.demon.co.uk**

LETTERS

LEVIATHAN

Dear Peter,

Your words of support for Leviathan in the autumn *Poetry Review* were greatly appreciated, but one small misunderstanding needs clarifying. Leviathan can't claim to be publishing Giles Goodland's first collection: that honour went to Oversteps Books when they did his first book-length sequence *Littoral* in 1996 (still available).

Yours,

MICHAEL HULSE
Amsterdam

SOME CONTRIBUTORS

Smita Agarwal's poems appear in Eunice de Souza's *Nine Indian Women Poets*, reviewed on p.3.

Patience Agbabi's *Transformatrix* was reviewed in Vol 90 No3, p.24.

Rafael Alberti (1902-1999) was one of Spain's leading twentieth-century poets, one of the generation of '27.

Gillian Allnutt's *Lintel* is forthcoming from Bloodaxe in 2001.

Sujata Bhatt's new collection *Augatora* is just out from Carcanet.

Peter Bland's *Selected Poems* are published by Carcanet.

Buddhadeva Bose (1908-74) is a major Bengali poet of the 20th century.

Paula Burnett is the Editor of *The Penguin Book of Caribbean Verse*.

Stephen Burt's first collection. *Popular Music*, was published in the USA by CLP/Colorado in 2000.

Harry Clifton's prose book *On the Spine of Italy* (Pan) is out in paperback.

Julia Copus's frst collection, *The Shuttered Eye*, was published by Bloodaxe in 1995.

Fred D'Aguiar's *An English Sampler: New and Selected Poems* is due from Chatto in May.

Ketaki Kushari Dyson is preparing a Selected Poems edition of Buddhadeva Bhose's poetry in English translation.

Ruth Fainlight's latest collection is *Sugar-Paper Blue* (Bloodaxe, 1997).

Elaine Feinstein's *Gold* was published by Carcanet in 2000.

Catherine Fisher's latest collection is *Altered States* (Seren, 1999).

John Goodby's *Irish Poetry Since 1950* was published by Manchester University Press in 2000.

John Greening's *Nightflights: New and Selected Poems* was published by Rockingham in 1999.

Vona Groarke's latest collection is *Other People's Houses* (Gallery, 1999).

Philip Gross's *Changes of Address: Poems 1980-1998* is due from Bloodaxe in 2001.

Mark Halliday's latest collection is *Selfwolf* (University of Chicago Press).

Fay Hart is an American poet now living in London.

Douglas Houston's latest collection is *The Welsh Book of the Dead* (Seren, 1999).

David Kennedy was a co-editor of *The New Poetry* and is the editor of *The Paper*, a new magazine devoted to innovative poetries.

John Kinsella's latest collection is *The Hierarchy of Sheep* (Bloodaxe).

Khan Singh Kumar's poems have appeared in *London Magazine, Poetry London* and *The Rialto*.

Hugh Macpherson was shortlisted for the Geoffrey Dearmer Prize in 1999.

E. A. Markham's latest collection is *Marking Time* (Peepal Tree, 1999).

Tanure Ojaide's latest collection is *Invoking the Warrior Spirit* (Africa World Press, 1999).

Helen Oswald has published in *The Rialto, London Magazine, Poetry London* and *Reactions*.

Stephanos Papadopoulos's first collection is forthcoming from Leviathan.

Greg Partridge is a journalist in Atascadero, California.

Jem Poster's new collection *Brought to Light* will be published by Bloodaxe in July.

Justin Quinn's second collection, *Privacy* (Carcanet), was published in 1999. He is an editor of *Metre*.

Phil Ramage posts reviews on Amazon.

Robert Saxton's first collection *The Promise Clinic* was published Enitharmon in 1994.

George Szirtes' latest collection is *The Budapest File* (Bloodaxe).

Jonathan Treitel was shortlisted for the Geoffrey Dearmer Prize.

Marc Tritsmans is a leading Dutch poet.

Ian Tromp reviews for various magazines, including *PN Review*.

Sarah Wardle won the Geoffrey Dearmer Prize in 1999.

Graeme Wright is a member of the Bridgewater Hall Writers Group in Manchester.

CORRECTION

In Martha Kapos's biographical note (Vol 90 No 3, p.81,the title of her Many Press pamphlet should read *The Boy Under the Water*.

PBS EXCLUSIVE BOOK SUPPLY SERVICE

Readers of *Poetry Review* can receive the UK-published books featured in the magazine post-free from the Poetry Book Society. If your local bookshop's idea of a poetry section is a shelf of Keats *Collected* and two tatty copies of *The Waste Land* this is what you've been waiting for! Call 020 8870 8403 between 9.30am and 5.30pm Mon-Fri to make your order, quoting "*Poetry Review*". All major credit/debit cards accepted, including Switch.

ADVERTISING

For details on how to advertise in *Poetry Review* visit www.poetrysoc.com/news/adrates.htm or contact marketing@poetrysoc.com. Telephone 0207 420 9895